D1625359

AN ECLECTIC EEL

Other books by Dalton Camp

Gentlemen, Players and Politicians
Points of Departure

AN ECLECTIC EEL

BY
DALTON CAMP

DENEAU
PUBLISHERS
& COMPANY LTD.

• OTTAWA •

Canadian Cataloguing in Publication Data

Camp, Dalton, 1920-
  An eclectic eel
ISBN 0-88879-068-6
1. Canada—Politics and government—1968-
1979.* 2. Canada—Politics and government—
1979-1980.* I. Title.
FC625.C35   320.971   C81-090142-0
F1034.2.C35

ISBN 0-88879-068-6

©Deneau Publishers & Company Ltd.
  281 Lisgar Street
  Ottawa, Ontario K2P 0E1
  Canada

Printed in Canada by John Deyell Company

Contents

Acknowledgments

Apart from the Introduction, all these articles and reviews have been published previously in various Canadian newspapers and magazines, including: *Atlantic Insight, The Globe & Mail, The Montreal Gazette, The Montreal Star, Report Magazine, Saturday Night, The Toronto Star* and syndicate, *The Toronto Sun* and syndicate, *Toronto Telegram.* Their tacit acceptance of the republication of these pieces is gratefully acknowledged.

For Aurilla Sanborn Camp

"Like eels at the bottom of the fish barrel,
they keep them all awake up there."
Anon.

A reader of mine thought this simile, which he had come across in the British press, suitably described the role of the political columnist. Hence, the title of this book — a collection of columns, lighter essays and reviews, most of which first saw the light of day in newspapers or magazines over a period of time as yet too recent to be historic. I daresay, except for members of my immediate family, many will read most of them as original material.

As for "eclectic" — to spare anyone looking it up — it is, of course, a play on the word describing a genus of eel, but means, for my purposes, "selecting such doctrines as pleased him in every school. . . not exclusive in opinion, taste, etc.," as defined by Oxford. Put otherwise, it is hoped there will be something here for almost everyone.

Having dispensed with the *éclaircissement* as to title, I should offer some further explanation about the book itself. You will find it, I trust, an easy book to put down; it was so intended. Were I obliged to unveil a marketing plan, I would say it could have been especially produced for people who travel by air, those who, of necessity, read in fits and starts, between Toronto and Montreal, for example, or Vancouver and Calgary.

After much experience and observation, I have concluded that air travel considerably increases literary consumption. It is no secret that many air travellers, when aloft, would sooner read than eat, which alone may account for the impressive numbers of them found foraging among the racks in airport bookstores. But reading on the wing, so to speak, demands a certain kind of book, which, for the average reader, is a tome of medium-to-light heft, preferably one which can be read either from front to back, or in reverse, or even at random; the reader need never worry about losing his place or the author's narrative thread.

Travelling with the proper book in hand also provides blessed distraction for those who otherwise would find themselves attuned to redundant oxygen-mask demonstrations, the mysterious fluctuations of Rolls-Royce engines, the groaning of flaps, and bleak, unrewarding conversation with garrulous strangers. These are only a few of the compelling reasons for producing *An Eclectic Eel*.

For most of us, writing in Canada, about Canada, for Canadian eyes, takes considerably more time and effort than, in any material sense, it is worth. Any cost-benefit study of the life of a writer in these parts would be brutally discouraging for those who imagine they might prosper from such a career. But most who write, do so out of compulsion; very few are qualified to do anything else. I have sometimes experienced twinges of sympathy for book publishers, their editors, and, occasionally, even for booksellers, but never for writers. They are, after all, doing what they like, a rarity in this world only to be envied.

The columnist is, of course a peculiar variant of the writer; obviously it is possible to be a columnist and not be a writer at all — present-day examples abound. It is also possible to moonlight as a columnist, as do a number of political figures, professional economists, medical doctors, and corporate executives, among others. The afternoon newspaper I read boasts more columnists than Winfield Farms has horses, and, as to subject matter, about everything from advice to the lovelorn to instruction for the prime minister of Canada.

Political columnists specialise in the latter. We are all possessed of our own opinions, arrived at out of our own experience, enriched by our own sources, and embroidered by our own bias. And we do offer advice, usually in the guise of criticism, knowing it to be gratuitous and almost certain to go unheeded. The columnist is like a witch-doctor without a tribe, or a member of a party of one, lacking either followers or adherents. All he can claim to have are readers, of whom few, if any, are devout.

Those who write on politics, including the allegedly detached purists, are informants of one sort or another; but, however informative, they are all fundamentally purveyors of their own opinions. Information does not appear to be as important to the reader as is the quality and vigour of the opinion expressed. Newspapers serve to satisfy the need to know; columnists serve merely to satisfy a curiosity as to their opinion. It is possible to be interesting but not informative, also possible to be informative and unread.

The function of the columnist, as I believe it to be, is to offer another and different opinion, which, ideally, will be his own and also provocative — sufficient, at least, to stimulate second thoughts. H.L. Mencken, the original American curmudgeon, once defined the columnist's role as that of comforting the afflicted and afflicting the comfortable. This is difficult to achieve in a country such as Canada where the truly comfortable are imperturbable and the truly afflicted are inconsolable. My own purposes have been less ambitious.

One's political opinion is coloured by one's perception of Canadian politics. It has lately seemed to me that the greatest hazard to the writer on politics in Canada is the risk of taking the subject too seriously. It is possible to view any of our transient crises, however alarming, as being less than terminal in their implications. But there is a recurrent incantation in our politics, resembling that of the final game of the playoffs, which insists that, should something or other happen, "there's no tomorrow." I have myself sometimes been lulled or goaded into a similar confusion, each time living to regret it.

The state of politics, like that of everything else, has changed dramatically since I began my apprenticeship in the late 1940s. As to how much, it would be as easy to ask a general practitioner how much the state of medical practice has changed in the same period. The difference, however, between the changes in politics and in medicine could be expressed more simply in terms of their effect upon the politically involved citizen and upon the individual patient. Clearly, the patient is better off; the citizen is certainly not.

Since the advent of television, the role of political parties has been steadily eroded. Election campaigns have become electronic campaigns, shifting the emphasis from what was said to what is seen — from oratory to image, information to illusion. It is a novel condition, one in which no one *listens* while everyone *looks*: Nixon sweats, Muskie weeps, Stanfield stumbles (or fumbles), Diefenbaker shakes, Clark quakes; politics has become a spectator sport.

Onlooking is an act of sublimation, a concession by the observer that, while he may have an interest in the proceedings, he has no real part to play in them. Still, a spectator with end-zone seats may believe — with reason — that his and others' lusty exhortations in support of the home team could inspire the players to exceed themselves in their efforts. But for the televiewer such participation is impossible: his team may win or lose, people may die before his very eyes, yet the parade of events passes before him governed by the random choice of accident. Unable to be heard, how can he care?

Alienation is not a regional phenomenon, but a continental one. The further the citizens retreat into their armchairs and the longer they glower at the magic lantern, the more they become spectators to the demise of the party system. (Already, I suspect, the thought is anti-climactic.)

The answer to the problem, obviously, is not to curtail the success of viewers to the medium. Who needs a revolution? But I am struck by this curious coincidence of the slowly declining rate of voter turn-out in Canadian elections, and the more rapidly declining rate of turn-out in the United States, with the heavy — not to say, excessive — use of television by the political parties in both countries in their election campaigns and, according to all evidence, with the concomitant decline of the role of the parties in the political process.

The danger to democracy has always been the danger of an electorate seized by passivity. The threat to the primacy of the parties in the political process, at the beginning of the television age, was from the para-political movements (those against the Vietnam war, for women's rights, the counter-culture) which would be co-opted. But now the threat is widespread spectatorism, alienation and bleak resignation, all encouraged by the central role of television in our lives.

I have asked myself if the fact that British voters are still motivated to vote their interest bears any relation to the limited access of that country's political parties to the medium of television. Certainly I question the wisdom, if such it be, of encouraging the most complex and decisive of our institutional processes, which is politics, to conduct its election campaigns in the most simplistic yet compelling of the media — television.

Those who manage the party organizations these days have seized upon the medium as though it were nirvana. It is the perfect medium for manipulation, the ideal environment in which to sell sedatives and pain-killers. But the managers are blameless, since they are only using the available technology in precisely the way it must be used. For them to do otherwise would simply be irresponsible. It is interesting, nonetheless, to see how the political system itself has been redesigned to accommodate the demands of electronic campaigning; because the extensive use of television is lavishly expensive, both in production costs and the purchase of time, the parties no longer finance their own campaigns from conventional sources. The taxpayers do.

In the 1980 federal election, the three major parties declared expenditures totalling $11.3 million for "advertising, travel, and office costs." Of this amount, they were directly reimbursed with $2.75 million out of the federal treasury (some $500,000 more than for the same purposes in the election the previous year!). Furthermore, *most* of the remaining monies raised and spent by the parties came from contributions for which tax-credits were allowed, again at the expense of the federal treasury. And, of course, the largest single expenditure by far of these considerable sums went for television advertising.

Both the managers and their charges, the politicians, know what they're doing. Whether any of them have any philosophical doubts about the wisdom of what they're doing, or recognize its profound effect upon the political process, is doubtful. To begin with, their's is a reactive function, not a reflective one. But as long ago as 1968, Joe McGinniss, reporting on the packaging of Richard Nixon for the television age, described the purposeful process exactly: "Keep the people on the other side of the screen."

In Canada, we did not start that way; it is ironic to recall how we did begin to employ the new medium, and why we soon came to adopt the Nixonian process. In the beginning, the parties were not allowed to purchase time on television. Allotted free time, they could fill it only with identified spokesmen (no faceless crowds) who were allowed only to speak (no technical animation) — the so-called bare "face-in-the-window." The trouble with all this swiftly became apparent to the parties, as it did to the CBC and the regulatory bodies: if the format was right for politics, it was wrong for television. The ratings were disastrous; the viewer wanted to *watch*, not listen.

The solution to the problem then appeared obvious: if the parties were to use television, it would have to be on television's terms. There were some who thought the salvation lay in televised political debates. They were wrong. The classic structure of the debate is based upon argument between pro and con, one view against another and upon one resolution. Debates involving third parties call for elaborate stratagems, and were ornately complicated. Debates involving four parties were simply chaotic: one of the most hilariously irrelevant exercises in the history of political television must have been the "debate" in 1968 between Pierre Trudeau, Robert Stanfield, Tommy Douglas and Real Caouette.

Anyway, it soon proved impossible to secure the willingness of the parties to participate. After the disaster of 1968, one party or another declined the invitation — until 1979, when Joe Clark, P.E. Trudeau and Ed Broadbent were prevailed upon, each accepting the opportunity for his own extraneous reason.

That experience, however, proved enough for the Liberals to discourage their participation in the 1980 campaign. Besides, the managers had long since reduced the art of electronic electioneering to thirty- and sixty-second commercials, judged to be within the tolerable limits of the average viewer's attention span for sanitized political material. The parties had the people where they wanted them — on the other side of the screen.

The enormity of television's impact upon the institutions of society is immeasurable, if only because there is not yet an end to it, only a continuing, deepening process of cause and effect. How can one measure the impact of the medium which has made the afternoon, for example, a killing ground for newspapers? To say that television has made all politics presidential, or driven general magazines and afternoon papers to the wall, is so commonly accepted a fact as to have become trite. But television has done considerably more and is still doing so.

Because it demanded increasingly heavy dollops of money, television "reformed" political financing to give the parties significantly greater resources to purchase not only television time but people and techniques, including computerized direct mail and public opinion research. As a result, while the present-day party cadres are very well paid and highly professionalized, voluntarism is all but dead.

The rank-and-file of the parties, once considered to represent an omnibus of interests, have become competing factions acting on behalf of special or regional interests. Their usefulness in the political process is rapidly decreasing. They too perceive the system as presidential; they too think of politics in the same simple or detached terms as do non-partisans. Politics, which once inspired group loyalty and avid commitment, now arouses a consuming interest in techniques and in endless critical evaluations of leadership suitability as deduced from television performance. Were it not for private ambition or patronage interests, anarchy would be certain.

The compulsion of the party managers to poll public opinion, reduce the findings to the broadest common denominators, and trivialize them for the exclusive benefit of those on the other side of the screen may be said to be merely the politics of old, now projected and magnified to some mega-factor. After all, there were always slogans, crudely condensed argument, and trappings designed for mass appeal. Still, the pageantry was incidental and meant to stir the blood, not tranquillize the mind. Radio, a logical extension of the public platform, commanded the ear, provoked its own imagery, and rendered inert the listener's involvement.

It is ironic that as the methods and means of communication have vastly increased, those with whom the parties are communicating have increased *their* distance. The political party, for all its new-found affluence and expertise, is a withering institution, becoming an artefact in the society it once tempered and shaped.

Those directly involved in the parliamentary system know this themselves. They have, indeed, seen it coming. I do not believe it coincidental that, as the influence of the party system wilted, the phenomenon of incumbency flowered. Partisanship has been essential to parliamentary democracy, the ins and the outs playing identifiable roles, seated opposite. But, once again, unmistakable changes have occurred which, cumulatively, have liberated elected members from the constraints of party loyalty, freed them from the discipline of leader and caucus, and make them no longer members of a political party but more like political entrepreneurs.

The bureaucratization of the party organizations has been complemented by the bureaucratization of Parliament. Members' indemnities, pensions, allowances and perquisites have been considerably increased in recent years, along with the provision of more personal staff, constituency offices, and "free" transportation, postal and telephone services. I shall not dwell on this subject, since there is more written about it elsewhere in these pages. Enough to say that the new circumstances Members of Parliament have created for themselves were designed to strengthen the prospects of *all* for prolonging their incumbency, this in itself constituting a conspiracy against the purposes of the party system. Further, while it has always been accepted that a majority of elected members of any House at any time were disposable, given their uneven abilities, we are now seeing a concentrated effort to make them indisposable.

All this may help to explain the fragmenting of the national parties into disputatious factions of the regions. The inevitable consequences, it seems to me, are an increasing polarization and alienation out of which consensus becomes impossible. The strains upon a democracy when the parties fail to perform their essential unifying task are considerable and they will not be eased merely by changing leaders, or even governments, but only by a recognition of the need to restore the party system.

It may be said that I myself have had a hand in all this, as "image-maker," publicist and propagandist. Admittedly, I was among those strongly opposed to the original regulations which limited the uses of television for partisan purposes. A lot of us were wrong, because none of us knew enough about the monster we were dealing with — not even the CBC. We thought it was radio with pictures; it wasn't. Now that we know better, we may have to live with the consequences of that hasty, uninformed and fateful judgment. As it has turned out, television was not the nirvana, but Pandora's box. In the meantime, as one with a long apprenticeship in politics — and a residual, lasting respect and affection for the system — I consider myself fortunate to have the opportunity to *write* about politics, in the hope, however forlorn or grandiose, of occasionally encouraging participation and provoking readers into "the insurgency of thought." I admit to my concern with

xvii

the decline of healthy partisanship, the homogenization of issues, the rise of factionalism, and the increase in personal venom and bitterness so uncharacteristic of a parliamentary democracy.

The concern may sometimes lead to excessive opinion, if not in my judgment, then in that of others. In the last federal election, I thought the Liberal strategy and campaign not only unprecedented but undemocratic. I said as much in a column which went "on the spike" at the *Toronto Star*, after which the *Star* and I parted company. The column has been reprinted in this book: I cannot say that I would change a word of it, other than to improve upon its emphasis.

I would be happy to see television used more sparingly, not in the self-interest of the party managers and politicians, but in the urgent needs of the party system. Given the powers of a John Meisel, I would prohibit the commercial use of the medium but provide frequent opportunity for debate among the leaders, inviting them to ventilate their views and positions, or lack of them, or quit television altogether. It would, at least, represent an effort to elevate the message over the medium; perhaps it would also rescue citizen involvement from the clutch of apathy. Almost certainly, it would signal the restoration of the party system.

The reason, after all, why the parties are in such disrepair is because the leaders and the cadres have no real interest in them. While it is always desirable to maintain an efficient party organization in the familiar manner, it is no longer necessary to do so. With the efficacy of polling, given unlimited access to television, and with financial underwriting by the taxpayer — who needs a political party?

Sensibly, we have to doubt the prospects of change and improvement. We are dealing with politicians and party managers, not with choirs of angels, and they are not about to give up what is, for them, a good thing. From a marketing, packaging and promotion point of view, it *is* a good thing — neat, manageable and predictable — none of which can be said about political parties.

It is perhaps something I have taken too seriously, another in a list of private concerns one raises in public to the chorus of "Who cares?" So it all comes back to the function of the columnist, who is among the hardy few left who are still working at communicating thought and opinion on politics through the written word, without benefit of animation or illustration.

This hardly suggests that the words are cast in bronze or are suitable for framing. Many of them are written on the winds. But I have been persuaded that some of the pieces which follow might prove interesting, entertaining or insightful enough to bear their repetition at least once more. If the notion proved irresistibly flattering to the author, it was also complimentary to the reader, since it is rooted in the belief that politics is still an adventure of the mind.

Cambridge, New Brunswick
1 October 1981

The Media Watch
(continued)

18 February 1977

Senator Keith Davey could have been right, a painful enough concession for anyone to make but even more wrenching for me because, at the same time, I could have been wrong.

It will be remembered that one of the senator's antidotes for the ills of Canadian journalism, as diagnosed by a Senate committee under his gavel, was the immediate construction of more schools of journalism. At the time, I scoffed.

Well, doubts now assail me. I don't think anyone should be allowed to practise in the media until they have spent at least sixteen years in journalism schools, which is equivalent to a jail sentence and perhaps unnecessarily harsh, but deserved, in my opinion, for what they are inevitably to inflict upon their readers.

To give impetus to the Davey proposal, I am establishing a scholarship for the *Toronto Star*'s legislative correspondent, Jonathan Manthorpe. Forthwith. Writing beneath the beguiling headline, "[Ontario] MPPs badly need $2,400 pay raise," Manthorpe offers the following:

"... a gentleman named Dalton Camp... was chairman of the Ontario Commission of the Legislature... The Members dearly hoped Camp would... recommend a healthy pay raise... but Camp failed them. The commission did recommend a number of improvements for MPPs, such as more staff and so forth, but on the oh so tender subject

1

of pay, he [that's me] throws it right back in the politicians' court, saying only there was a need for a review and adjustment of indemnities and allowances."

Au contraire, as they say in Alberta. The only thing the Camp Commission threw at the politicians was money: $3,000 more in annual indemnity; $1,500 more in tax-free allowance; a new $3,000 accommodation allowance for out-of-town members; free air, rail and bus transportation; increased automobile allowances; severance pay for defeated members; chauffeured limousines for all party leaders, and other treats.

The pay increases represented a boost of 25 percent over the then existing rates and were, in absolute terms, more than the $2,400 which is now "badly needed." In the judgment of some, we were too generous. Manthorpe only says we fudged the issue and passed the buck back to the Members; presumably, given the same standard of accuracy, he would report the Second Coming as Armageddon and put down the difference to editorial interpretation.

The *Globe and Mail*, in more contemporary vein, published a story from its Edmonton correspondent on the recent Jack Horner roast at which, reads the report, "tension developed when Bryce Mackasey and Donald Camp [sic] exchanged insults." While wondering what cousin Donald was doing at the roast, my eye fell on a clarification which identified the Camp in question as "the Tory back-room organizer and political columnist."

So it wasn't cousin Donald after all. Still, it has been a long time since this political columnist organized a back room, although I have recently rearranged the furniture in my Jemseg, N.B., bunker. Given a few years in one of Keith Davey's journalism schools, the *Globe*'s Edmonton correspondent might have been trained to describe me, more accurately, as "the former Tory back-room organizer, Horton Academy rugby captain, and recent contributor to the *Globe and Mail* book review section."

But it is not true that I exchanged insults with Mackasey, not at all. I merely provided the spectators at the Horner roast with a résumé of Mackasey's political career, which included the near-bankruptcy of the Unemployment Insurance Commission under his stewardship, the frequent shutdown of the post office during his ministry, and the collapse of the Bourassa government in Quebec shortly after Mackasey ventured into the province to save it. It is surely no fault of mine that the audience thought this hilarious.

Mackasey, however, was not so amused, his sense of humour having, for some reason, been temporarily impaired. He did, true enough, say insulting things about me, all of which I cheerfully endured, since it was a revelation to the Tories in Alberta to learn that I could provoke Grits as well as Conservatives.

However, I am loathe to allow Mackasey's somewhat mordant version of the event to stand uncontested. According to Canadian Press, which is possibly the largest journalism school we have, Mackasey was merely trying to save confederation. I sat through the entire Horner roast and never suspected confederation was in any real danger, but then Bryce and I were at opposite ends of the table and he may have had a better view of things.

He did say, according to CP, that he felt "Confederation is too serious a matter to be brought up at such an occasion on a humorous level."

Such a sentiment, albeit pontifical, is worthy of the stoutest federalist, and Mackasey's one-man mission to save confederation commends him. Still, since it permits him to describe Albertans as citizens of "the second separatist province," and myself as lacking "the guts to fight for Canada," it does seem that some of us, at least, ought to be permitted to take it lightly. Indeed, so far as the Horner roast went, it could be said that Mackasey committed an act of self-immolation.

The trouble with journalism — getting back to Senator Davey — is that it reports things that didn't happen (the Manthorpe School), or more than happened (as with the *Globe*'s correspondent), or a good deal less than what happened (as with Canadian Press). Class dismissed.

1 November 1979

Question: We have in our studios today Mr. Dalton Camp, syndicated columnist, sometime author, and former Conservative éminence grise. Mr. Camp, we understand you have written a book which is due in the bookstores any day now?
Answer: Well, if you don't mind a self-serving answer — yes. The title of the book is *Points of Departure*, published by Deneau & Greenberg, Ottawa, and the price is $14.95, which is slightly less than a tank of gas for the average family car.
Q.: Perhaps you could tell our listeners, Mr. Camp, how this book came to be written?
A.: This book came to be written because Messrs. Deneau and Greenberg came to me and asked me to write it. They believed the recent federal election would be, in their term, "a watershed" in our political history and that I might be able to confirm their opinion with a few well-chosen words. Since I admired both their perspicacity and their pluck, I agreed to try.

Q.: We heard from Larry Zolf that there are some big words in your book, Mr. Camp. How come you use big words?

A.: Mr. Zolf once wrote a book based upon the word "dialectic," which means "dealing with metaphysical contradictions," which has to do with "the theoretical philosophy of being and knowing." I didn't have to understand any of that to enjoy Zolf's book. I believe the English language is there to be used. For me, at least, using the language is a good part of the pleasure of writing. I think we should be stretched a little, if we're strong enough to sit down and read a book. Otherwise, we can more easily communicate by grunts and grimaces and by saying, "Heavy, man, y'know, like wow." But when people express themselves like that, you never know whether they're saying there has been a death in the family or someone has won a lottery.

Q.: Why did you write your book in the third person?

A.: Well, of the three sections in the book, two are written in the third person and the other in the first person. But as I explained in the prologue I wrote most of it in the third person because I felt like it — like a third person, that is — when I sat down to write it. After all, everyone has more than one dimension, even though we are all stereotypes in the minds of others. Observing P.E. Trudeau, I sometimes think there are seven of him, one for every day of the week. Writing in the third person is one way of warning the reader not to be too cocksure that he grasps what you're saying and why, simply because he knows who you are. It's a defence against too much presumption.

Q.: Your book has been billed as "controversial." What does that mean?

A.: I guess it means that some will take exception to parts of it. It also means — getting back to stereotypes — that when one is considered to be controversial, one is expected to fulfil that expectation, whether it's a book or a comment on the weather.

Q.: How about the critics and reviewers? What do they think about *Points of Departure*?

A.: So far, so good, with both authorized and unauthorized reviews. One must anticipate the inevitable harvest of nits and the usual reviews by some who will never have read the book. When this is over, I am writing a piece on "The Politics of Books and of Book Reviews," which I shall offer as a guide to those who read either of them. There is, for example, one newspaper publisher who said he would refuse to do anything to promote a book for "that s.o.b. Camp." Since he is a man who has made a fortune by publishing a newspaper for people who can't read, I am not sure he could have been helpful in any case. And then there's the bookstore in Toronto that will not stock it because — well — because of the Diefenbaker business, y'know what I mean?

Q.: So your book has become controversial even before it's in the bookstores?

A.: I am already preparing the bunker for the siege. But I do have to say that those who have seen the galleys of the book — my relatives, the hardy toilers at Deneau & Greenberg, and a couple of politicians — all have generously allowed as to how reading it made them laugh and made them mad, nearly at the same time. A struggling author can't ask for more.

Q.: Thank you, Mr. Camp.

A.: Not at all.

8 November 1979

Terence Macartney-Filgate, known to me for some years as plain Terry Filgate, was kind enough to invite me to a preview of *Dieppe 1942*, an invitation I accepted with alacrity, since the whole stupifying horror of that peculiarly Canadian enterprise during World War II has long since, believe it or not, become incorporated into a personal political philosophy.

The essence of that philosophy is simply a question: "But what if they're wrong?" Which is to say, by way of explanation: such is the legitimate query one ought to ask of all the grand designs proposed by those who have command or governance over our lives. It's a good question, you could say, for Gerald Bouey and the Bank of Canada, or for the promulgators of the policy for privatizing PetroCan, or, indeed, for the sponsors of separatism in Quebec. The salient fact in much of our history, or anyone else's, is that the more crucial the policy or plan, the more human folly there will be in it; the stupidity quotient increases in direct proportion to the size of the enterprise.

Some will say, of Filgate's film, that it only confirms Sherman's aphorism that war is hell. No doubt about it, *Dieppe 1942* reconfirms that, in the spades, you might say, of gravediggers. General Dollard Menard, of the Fusiliers de Montréal, avers that "wars have produced nothing but misery," an absolution which becomes a man who was there. But perhaps the reflection on Dieppe by John Godfrey, then a Spitfire pilot and now a senator, is the most pertinent: "People excused Dieppe by saying, 'Well, we learnt by our mistakes.' Well, we didn't need to make the mistakes we made at Dieppe."

Of course not. But the trouble with war — one among a number — is that, whether things go wrong or go right, you can still get killed. At Dieppe, where nothing went right, the slaughter was not so much the penultimate example of the horror of war but a terminal comment on the stupidity of men endowed with power of command for which they were manifestly unfit. That they could also be decent, honour-

5

able, well-intentioned and even the very best we had, does not, alas, make them any brighter.

But it would be merely facile to say they were an example of "the military mentality," when it is a more wholesome truth that they were a fateful example of the human tendency to equate one's rank and station in life with one's cerebral capacity. Any one of the dead awash in the tides at Dieppe could have conceived a better strategy for the assault than the one handed down from Combined Operations Headquarters; it is, at least, inconceivable that a lance-corporal could have done any worse.

Which leads me to Lord Louis Mountbatten, whom Filgate employs to pronounce the benediction on Dieppe: "Without Dieppe," Lord Louis says, with the familiar imperturbability of all great commanders, "we couldn't possibly have had the invasion. Without the invasion we couldn't possibly have won the war." Neither statement, of course, is remotely true. But without Mountbatten, we might possibly not have had Dieppe.

Among those present at the screening of *Dieppe 1942* was Brigadier Lord Lovat, whose commandos were also involved in the operation, although mercifully not on the beaches. Called upon to say a few words, Lovat did so. I thought his testimony had the perfect ring of truth: "The utter sheer folly of Dieppe," was his description of the event. "Let's face it. It was for no good purpose."

After the film, Filgate said to me that he would be interested in the reaction of those who would see it who had no personal recollections of the second world war — the nineteen year-olds, for example. So would I.

Filgate, his associates, and the CBC merit our commendation, since the film is one of those rare and special enterprises which dignifies and celebrates the mandate of the mother corporation.

But I hope the nineteen year-olds who see the film will not believe it to be a statement on the folly of war, although it is. Better that they also come away from it with their scepticism re-enforced, and that they realize the perversions of judgment which so often infect all those who have power, authority and governance over their lives. The most dangerous presumption in a free society is the one which allows that our leaders know what they're doing. The slaughter of the young on the beaches of Dieppe remains forever an obscenity, but less so perhaps if, when reminded of it, we remember to ask the question.

Hugh Sidey, who writes (for *Time Magazine*) one of the most perceptive columns found anywhere, recently reported the thesis of a Duke University professor, James David Barber, on the subject of the American presidency.

"A revolution is under way," writes Professor Barber. "No longer do the Democratic and Republican standard-bearers control the choice of standard-bearers. In their place a new set of king-makers has arisen: the journalists. For it is in the newspapers, the magazines and on television that the presidential candidates are created and destroyed."

Speaking as a onetime suspected king-maker, now retired, I admit to having said as much myself lately, not only about the American presidency, but about our own Canadian political system, which has itself come to be presidential. Even so, I have begun to doubt the thesis and to suspect both Professor Barber and myself would have difficulty brushing aside the gathering number of exceptions to it.

How to explain, for example, the romp being made of the present Republican primary race by that septuagenarian, Ronald Reagan, a politician disliked, mistrusted and scorned by nearly every American journalist left of William F. Buckley and George Will?

Still, Reagan's near certain nomination as his party's leader does not dissuade Professor Barber from insisting that "If [a presidential candidate] has his priorities straight, he is first and foremost a seeker after favourable notice from the journalists who can make or break his progress."

But such does not explain the failure of "the journalists" to launch the candidacy of a Reagan opponent, George Bush, whose hopes fluttered aloft in New Hampshire but have been grounded ever since. Nor the strenuous efforts of the *New York Times* to float Congressman John Anderson as a challenge to Reagan, exertions which have thus far produced only a handful of delegates.

Further, it is obvious the good professor has never heard of P.E. Trudeau, who, far from being "a seeker after favourable notice from the journalists," chose instead to ignore them altogether, achieving thereby a miraculous restoration.

Indeed, if favourable notices from the media counted for much, Richard Nixon could never have been elected president of the United States (twice), and, one could add, Ed Broadbent would have become the prime minister of Canada. For life. And what of Joe Clark? When the journalists mocked him, he won; when they empathized, he lost.

No, the empirical evidence points in the other direction: in the absence of party wheels, big city machines, and power brokers, who used to make or break a candidate, mass communications have not emerged "to fill virtually the whole gap in the electoral process," as Barber would have it. In fact, the evidence suggests that a bad press often helps; show me a politician the journalists don't like, and I'll be tempted to give odds on his winning.

I raise these matters to point to a paradox. In recent travels about the country, I have detected a considerable body of public opinion which subscribes to Barber's thesis (even though it's unaware of it) and to a further conviction that what is wrong with politics is the fault of the (expletive deleted) media, especially the (likewise) commentators. Despite all evidence to the contrary, an astonishing number of otherwise reasonable people believe there's nothing so much wrong with the politics and politicians as with the reportage of them. Even though, as they are at pains to say, they tend not to believe a word they read, or a voice they hear, either from the hustings or from the media.

We appear to have arrived somewhat past the point of a healthy scepticism but somewhere closer to an Age of Disbelief. In such times, it's hard to be a journalist, harder still a politician, and nearly impossible to be a professor.

31 August 1980

It was Black Wednesday just about everywhere, with deaths in the Canadian family — the *Ottawa Journal* and the *Winnipeg Tribune* — and now you can count the number of two-newspaper towns in this country on the fingers of one hand, comfortably. Were it not for the brash and bold *Toronto Sun*, and its ventures in Edmonton and Calgary, we'd be down to just three.

The daily newspaper is the last sacred cow in our society and we are all raised up from childhood in the belief that the press must not only be free but must seem to be free, and therefore newspapers, unlike anything or anyone else under the sun, must make their own way in the world without government patronage.

As the last bastion of free enterprise — unfettered, unencumbered, and untouched by the dead hand of the state — it is interesting to watch how things work. In a word, they work badly.

We can now stand back and examine this scale model of the free press operating in the free enterprise system and in the free marketplace. It turns out that this institution which we all revere, and without which our freedom, if not our very lives, would be at risk, is a loser. If printer's ink be the mother's milk to a free society, then a lot of children in Canada are going to go hungry. It's not because there's a shortage of milk, but it's only that the distributor can't afford to deliver the stuff. It comes as something of a jolt to realize, important as the free press is to us, that if someone couldn't afford it, we wouldn't have it. Wherefore there is no profit, therefore there is no free press. Amen.

Of course, nowhere is it written that there must be at least two newspapers in every market. Nor has it been established — so far — that if there were no newspapers we would all perish. As most of us rediscover every summer, it is possible to survive for several days without ever seeing a paper; indeed, some claim therapeutic benefits — like going into retreat — from a week of no news, comment, opinion, or morning smiles. Still, knowing there are newspapers out there is like knowing there's a fire department somewhere near — it's comforting.

Whenever I have journeyed behind the Iron Curtain — where, let it be said, newspapers do not disappear, although journalists sometimes do — what has always struck me as the singular difference between that society and our own is simply the lack of choice. It seems to me if you wished to consign someone to a dull, brutish existence, you would offer that person one of everything and two of nothing. Such is the problem of one-newspaper markets; no matter how good the product is, it's all there is, and we are all enervated by the lack of choice, another opinion, and other stimuli.

It seems to me we ought to sense the danger in this that has to do with more than the sudden death of venerable and reliable institutions. There is much more to this than mourning the loss. Our national condition is critical and we lack both the will and the ways to deal with it.

The Parliament of Canada fell all over itself in 1976 trying to appear graceful and correct in an effort to salvage the Canadian magazine industry. It conferred dual citizenship on *Reader's Digest*, expelled *Time Magazine*, and bestowed special status on *Maclean's*. There are as many opinions as there are copies of *Maclean's*, as whether the result has been profitable to the industry, or even to *Maclean's*.

The Canadian book publishing industry is in dreadful trouble and its flagship publishing house could not survive a day without continued government support. Nothing much, if anything, has ever come from the bright, cheerful assurances of television licencees of the wonders they would perform as to Canadian content, other than the constant whining that they would go broke trying to deliver.

But as to that, we are only leaping distances away from the time when technology will make the nostrums of Canadian broadcasting, Canadian content, and government regulation obsolete, which will leave CBC with its national dreams and a mandate become an absurdity.

We are running out of newspapers and even those who say the worst is over won't bet much on it. If the criteria for survival is the bottom line, and naught else, we are heading for the day when we'll not only have fewer newspapers, but fewer Canadian books, few if any

9

magazines, and a broadcasting system disgorging eternal reruns of life in America. Unless, of course, someone is prepared to put their money where our pride is.

Someone was saying the other day, of John Diefenbaker, that he was a great parliamentarian. This seems to have become the quintessential truth about the man; when all other hyperbole has been exhausted, what remains is the tribute to the "great Canadian parliamentarian," and very likely the last one as well. Should an even greater parliamentarian arrive on the scene at some future time, it is possible no one will notice.

In today's politics, being an outstanding parliamentarian is a lonely achievement, the sort of talent which, while publicly acknowledged, the public neither comprehends nor particularly values. It is something akin to having an exceptional gift for solitaire.

I have tried to imagine what the First Ministers' Conference a fortnight ago would have been like had the "great Canadian parliamentarian" been in the chair rather than Prime Minister Trudeau. It proved impossible.

Like most men with considerable forensic skills, Diefenbaker was not at his best sitting down. He had no style or voice suitable for speaking from a chair. Unless he was waxing anecdotal, he tended to wander off into verbosity; furthermore, he found it impossible to be in repose. P.E. Trudeau's glacial calm at the conference table is as right for the prying eye of television as Diefenbaker's continual fidgeting would have been disastrously wrong.

Television has created a breed of politician suitable to its needs. Those who cannot think sitting down, maintain their composure, and express themselves within the limits imposed by a 21-inch screen in family parlours are doomed. They may be fast on their feet but it will get them nowhere; in the new politics there is no place to stand. What used to be called the political arena is now a studio, and while Arthur Meighen saw the electorate of his day as a jury, Trudeau sees it for what it has become — an audience.

We have not yet fully realized the impact of television on politics, even though it commands the process and has usurped the role of its more familiar institutions, such as the legislatures and the parties themselves. President Carter has complained that one of his opponents in the current presidential campaign, John Anderson, is "primarily a creation of the press." The *New York Times*, more to the point, describes

Anderson as the first presidential candidate of "the Television Party." What they are both saying is that you don't need a political party any more to run for president and become a spoiler; all you need is access to the tube.

Of course, in the new parliaments of television — the network "debates" between contending leaders — the candidates do stand on their feet. But they don't make speeches and they don't debate. If Demosthenes were around these days, he wouldn't be perfecting his oratory speaking with stones in his mouth; he'd be learning what to do with his hands.

You and I are more aware of television's dominance of the political process than are most of the politicians — the ones standing out there waving their arms and preaching to the deaf. It's hard for a man raised on the effusions of Edmund Burke, and inspired by John Diefenbaker's legendary skills as a parliamentarian, to accept the modern reality of his trade: if you can't hack it in television, you're better off back home drawing up wills or carrying around a sample case.

So, you may ask, what is it all coming to? Well, down south maybe it's coming to Ronald Reagan and, within the laws of possibility, some future clone of a John Anderson — a man without a party, with a white mane, and maybe on horseback.

As for Canada, it's coming to someone who can use the camera to manipulate its audience as well, or better, than does the prime minister. It won't be Joe Clark, and it hurts to say it, because, you know, Clark is as good, or better, a parliamentarian than Trudeau four days out of five any week the House is sitting.

20 August 1981

We could have saved much time, expense and subsequent adrenalin in this second government-sponsored assault on newspapering in Canada had the Kent Commission not bothered with any delineation of the problems, since the solutions were apparent to begin with. I mean by that: if you think a private property becomes public property because the property is a newspaper, then there are really no problems — only solutions. Profundities, rationales, arguments, statistics, recitals of how the Swedes do things (I am convinced that if the Swedes legalized white slavery, the notion would take root instantly in thinking circles in Canada), homilies, pieties, and other dilations and declensions serve only to make one's teeth ache.

If you are convinced that concentration of newspaper ownership is a bad thing, the only good thing to do is de-concentrate it. The appropriate fiats of divestiture naturally must come from the principal confiscatory power in the land, namely the government of Canada. Where else?

If you believe that the quality of journalism in Canada is inadequate to the needs, you improve the quality of journalism by improving the quality of journalism schools, an idea which originated in the seminal mind of Senator Keith Davey, an early Canadian primitive in the media reformation movement. If you deem it essential that the wire services hire more reporters and send them to more places, you send public money to Canadian Press, whether it wants it or not. Is there any other way?

If newspapers are, for whatever reason, unable to "devote more of their resources to the provision of information," you give them tax credits, as a carrot: if they do not respond by providing more information, you apply a surtax, as a stick.

Since newspaper proprietors who also have other commercial, though less onerous, interests, clearly constitute a perceived threat to the journalistic independence and integrity of their editors-in-chief, many of whom are apparently notorious cowards, these shall henceforth be protected by a Canada Newspaper Act, which will require the proprietor to sign a contract with his editor-in-chief, guaranteeing him his editorial independence, integrity and well-being.

Further, should any newspaper proprietor fail to abide by the requirements of the Canada Newspaper Act, he will soon hear from the Press Rights Panel (an annex to the Human Rights Commission) and from his paper's own advisory committee, which, I forgot to mention, is set up to monitor the paper's performance (except for "individual" papers, which is to say, a paper owned by an individual with no other visible means of support), on the initiative of the chief justice of the province involved, who is mandated to see the committee is properly established. After that, two members of this committee are elected to a provincial press council, which is a conduit to the Press Rights Panel, which is, you will recall, the watchdog of the Canada Newspaper Act.

Are you still there?

The trouble with applying doctrinaire solutions to the problems — and admitted ones — of newspapers and newspaper ownership is that the solutions, even so bizarre as these, will solve the problems easily enough, but they will also destroy the inherent value of a free press.

A newspaper is of value in our society only because it is free, meaning free of the capricious or discretionary judgments of bureaucrats, governments, commissioners and boards of review. If a newspaper is not free to err, to be allowed its perversities, or to be simply crummy, but is instead obliged to be perfect in the eyes of God and

Tom Kent, then, whatever else, we no longer have a free press but a captive one.

Reading the Kent Commission's report was, to me, like sitting through a filming of "Raiders of the Lost Ark" — at the same time scary and funny. Wild assertions leap from the pages, startling in their emphatic assumption, endearing in their naïveté, and oftentimes just plain funny:

"Most journalists. . . believe that newspapers should set more audacious goals, get to the bottom of facts and events, go beneath the tip of the iceberg, grapple with difficult, complex, but important subjects, and expose them, explain them clearly to the public, bring out the deeper significance of events, in short, assume the responsibility of finding and publishing what the public should know. . . ."

God knows, too many publishers, editors and reporters talk like that when confronted by Royal Commissions, or addressing a Rotary luncheon. But not only do I doubt "most journalists" truly believe that stuff, I am certain most readers would be bored stiff by a newspaper of such audacious pretension.

The promulgation of gush, however, is most strenuous in those passages wherein the Commission strives to elevate the daily newspaper to a national trust: "newspaper publishing is. . . a solemn, serious, and essentially public responsibility," it quotes a retired publisher as saying. And soon after, a gem from the Commission's own pen: "Few industries are based on philosophical and moral principles as is the press." (I quickly thought of two additional industries so based: the aircraft industry and the makers of prophylactics.) But there's more: "As my father taught me," Michael Sifton is quoted as saying, "we have a democracy because we have a free press. We don't have a free press because we have a democracy."

The trouble I have with this easy rhetoric on the essentiality of newspaper responsibility is perhaps trifling, given the subject matter, but I think it's dangerous all the same. I cannot look upon the *Globe and Mail* as owing any responsibility to me (and vice versa), any more than I can believe there is a moral principle lurking somewhere in the bowels of the *Toronto Star*. And if Michael Sifton wants to believe the egg came before the chicken — that there was a free press before there was, say, a free parliament — I simply despair for newspaper proprietors and for their properties. They are offering themselves up for divestiture.

"Print, principally newspapers, determines society's agenda." This is another of the sayings of Senator Davey, raised to scripture by the Commission. It would be because newspapers determine the national agenda, are the genesis and guarantor of democracy, and "determine . . .what we think about" (Davey again) that we would need to pry them loose from their owners through the interfacing of a Canada Newspaper Act, a Press Rights Panel, resident vigilante committees, obligatory contractual arrangements between owner and editor as "detailed in the statute," along with a dispensary of carrots and an arsenal of sticks. But since none of that is true, none of this is necessary.

But we must, as I say, accept first all these glorious attributions to the powers of newspapers; having done so, the impulse becomes almost irresistible, at least in this country, to bring them under the baleful purview of government. In essence, the Kent Commission has concluded that the press is too important to be free, based in part on the testimony of the proprietors themselves.

There are, however, glints of commonsense in the report which glow in the surrounding murk. "We think," the commissioners say, "that the freedom of the press should continue to mean the freedom of the proprietor to do what he likes with his newspaper, *provided that newspaper is his principal property*. [Emphasis their's.] The resulting products may in some cases fall short of social responsibility, but it is better to live with these deficiencies than to take the risks involved in any practicable regulation of content standards."

As I told the Davey Commission eleven years ago, a man who owns a newspaper ought to be free to sell it, close it down, give it away, or burn it to the ground. Subject to the laws relating to libel, arson, public mischief, and the income tax act, a free press means freedom to publish or not to publish.

The Kent Commission has allowed as much, but gutted the principle espoused by denying the same freedom to a newspaper proprietor who also owns — say — a refinery. Social irresponsibility becomes, despite all that has gone before, a lesser sin, for which there is dispensation for some, purgatory for others. I have had to resist the feeling that this curious double-standard was meant as yet another snare — the landscape is littered with them — to trap the Irving press in New Brunswick. Indeed, the pursuit by the Davey and Kent Commissions of the Irvings reminds me of nothing so much as those hilarious cartoons of the coyote's frenzied and futile pursuit of the Roadrunner.

A novelty nonetheless, this nice distinction between the absolved socially irresponsible proprietor, however defined, who owns only a newspaper and another indicted proprietor, perhaps *less* socially irresponsible, who happens also to be into conglomerates. Notwithstanding, an exquisite splitting of hairs: "But it is one thing for society to accept the power, including the power to be deficient in social responsibility, that belongs to the proprietor of a particular newspaper as such. It is quite another matter to accept unconditionally the power of a proprietor for whom a newspaper is only part of his interests. . ."

"The Davey Commission," the commissioners remind us, "said eleven years ago that the newsrooms of most Canadian newspapers were boneyards of broken dreams. Our investigations lead us to think that there are fewer dreams to break. . . .This malaise is, in the Commission's view, part of the price we pay for conglomerate ownership."

It has been my own experience that journalists, when gathered around the water cooler, are indistinguishable from any one else who works for a living. They gripe. The Commission reports the complaints of a CP staffer, weary of "being tied down by routine, rewriting hourly radio news bulletins and processing sports scores." And what would he rather do? Well — "There's an awful lack of original and investigative reporting."

You bet there is. You bet there always was. But the conglomerates and the chains have not inhibited original and investigative reporting. Nor have they been the seedbed for broken dreams. "My life's dream has been a perpetual nightmare," Voltaire said. He never knew Roy Thomson . . . or Tom Kent either.

Some Hon. Members

1971

Edgar Benson's seasonally adjusted army of unemployed inflation-fighters continues to grow, mocking his prophecy that prosperity is just around the corner. Meanwhile, Himself continues to tour the hustings, basking in the approving smiles of his supporters, all of whom have jobs.

We have not had, since the beginning of the forties, so much of the work force idle, and we have not had, at any time I can recall, so few people who seem to care about it. But it might be true that the electorate has some deeper wisdom, as it might also be true that Mr. Benson's unfounded optimism might only be a simple lack of candour.

We have been warned for some time of the prospects for joblessness which the modern technology would create, and of the fact that more and more of the unskilled and semi-skilled would become redundant. In addition, we must surely have known of the consequences to the labour market when the new generation of job applicants began to flood it, as it is now doing.

At any rate, we have the present spectre of hordes of our youth roaming the streets of the cities and thumbing their way about the country. The general population seems to assume they are all university students on a summer's lark, although few of them are, and nearly all of them would prefer to have work.

The hastily improvised federal program, Opportunities for Youth, so-called, has hardly scratched the surface of the problem. Something is better than nothing, especially for those who got the something, but the program was elitist in its concept, dealing primarily with university students and, by nature, assisted many who least needed help.

What do you do with the greater numbers of the young who have had vocational or technical education in the school system and can find no jobs?

It seems to me that, long after Mr. Benson has been called up to the Senate,* the problem will still be with us. To alleviate it demands the abandonment of many existing programs, which have become feeble palliatives, and which include our present barbaric welfare policies.

In their place, the federal government, with its provincial partners, have to rethink the whole business of spending priorities and social policy.

First among these is the need for an incomes policy which, whether it is called guaranteed annual income or income incentive or whatever, will have the effect of providing every adult or family unit with adequate means.

Our attitude towards "welfare," and other social assistance and subsidy, has been shaped by the notion that any society such as ours has its casualties, including those who are too lazy to work, and a fluctuating number of persons who were simply victims of cyclical turns in a free enterprise economy.

All this rationale grew out of our sublime faith in the efficacy of a free-enterprise, competitive economic system. The faith was not misplaced, but the dogma now is at fault. For in such a system of private competition there are winners, who are visible consumers and who pay taxes. But there are also losers — as in any competition — who have now become an invisible host of unemployed and who get welfare, sporadically and in some arbitrary measure.

Such a system no longer works, as witness the fact that welfare is no longer going only to "the poor," as we knew them, but to thousands who want to work, and have worked much of their lives, and to youth, who have never worked and cannot find work to do.

Meanwhile, the contest between federal, provincial and municipal jurisdictions to finance their own competing priorities and overlapping programs is seriously eroding the middle class, creating a new class of tax-paying poor. It is trifling comfort to have the grudging relief from federal income tax recently doled out by Mr. Benson to lower income groups; the real iniquity remains hidden in indirect federal sales taxes, provincial sales taxes and municipal property taxes, which have become punishing to the majority, even if much of the revenue goes to essential services.

*Wrong. He went to the other Other Place — the Canadian Transport Commission.

17

In reality, we have a regressive system of taxation, by which the poor pay a significantly higher percentage out of income for taxes than do the affluent, even though they pay little or no tax on personal income.

What is needed is a form of tax rebate or credit from the federal government to the benefit of all taxpayers in the lower income groups, which would recognize their present plight. Such a policy would also allow the federal government to help finance the substantial cost of education, now being borne almost entirely by the provincial taxpayer and the municipal ratepayer.

Finally, until or unless automation turns about to create jobs rather than erase them, priority in social policy must be given to the growing numbers of jobless young.

Obviously, the new age of majority, which now is more commonly at eighteen, indicates that we are going to have a growing number of adults who will be unemployed, if not unemployable. It is imperative that society, meaning its governments, do far more about the phenomenon than merely improvise.

At the very least, educational programs need to become better adapted to meet present needs, another way of saying our educational institutions must become more accessible (which is another way of saying "free"). And surely society cannot for long endure the sight of nearly an entire generation nomadically roaming the countryside, thumbing rides down the road, which is by way of saying free, or cheap, transportation.

This is hardly inspiring reading, nor inspired prose. And no need to deny the costly implications. But we are kidding ourselves in blaming poor Edgar Benson for being a bad prophet. Better to condemn his government for its terrifying, blind indifference to the problems of a new age, which now is so much upon us that all who have eyes can see the urgent need for reform and new policy.

11 July 1974

For the Conservatives, the election results could hardly have been worse. It was not only that they lost, but who and what were lost. While the Tories won nearly a hundred seats, many of their best and brightest candidates went down to defeat. And, worst of all, it is all too likely that the party will also lose its leader, Robert Stanfield.

After the wake, and whenever sobriety returns to the party, it will dawn on the Tories that they are faced with a leadership crisis far greater than they had during the sixties. The immediate question is not how soon Stanfield can be persuaded to retire, but how long he can be persuaded to stay. Were I Stanfield, I would promise them to stay on only a day at a time.

For a dangerously long period of time, the party has enjoyed the seeming luxury of quantity in its parliamentary representation, but, even though it has had many able and articulate voices, it has not had acceptable heirs to the leadership. Any Tory who looked in the mirror on the day following the election and thought he saw an heir to Stanfield's leadership is so dangerously deluded as to be unfit for the office.

This is not to say that promise or possibility is not there. After all, not even Stanfield came to the task prepared for it, even after serving ten years as a provincial premier. The evidence also suggests that P.E. Trudeau was himself unready for the demanding role of leadership and very nearly threw himself out of office in 1972. Neither of them knew enough about the country, or enough about the parliamentary process, and both needed years to learn.

But the hard reality is that the leadership question needs time before acceptable answers can be found, if, indeed, there are answers.

The great irony, among many, is that Stanfield is more needed by his party than he ever was, because he is simply the only strength it has to assure stability and continuity. It could also be said that the country needs him as well, since the role and competence of the official opposition in Parliament is at least as important as the conduct of the new majority Liberal government.

Canadians will sooner or later recognize the uniquely admirable qualities of the Tory leader. Better late than never, I suppose, and no doubt too late to provide much comfort to Stanfield himself. The history of Stanfield in federal politics has been to bring an essential decency and moderation to national politics, which was desperately needed, even though continually undervalued and even recently despised. So whatever he does, it will be out of a characteristic sense of duty and responsibility and not because of any obligation he might feel for such as the electors of Ontario, for example, or for the lesser luminaries within his own party, for another.

The unrevealed truth about this election was Ontario's fixed perception of Stanfield as a leader and as an alternative to P.E. Trudeau. At the outset of the campaign, to the certain surprise and dismay of the Tory campaign managers, the polls in Ontario showed the Conservatives far behind the Liberals, and Stanfield trailing Trudeau in terms of leadership qualities.

Most of us believe the media, during the campaign, enforced the bias, damaging Stanfield every newsday and exalting Trudeau. And while the Conservative party actually improved its position during the campaign, and on election day as compared to its low starting-point, the perception of Stanfield improved hardly at all.

Indeed, so far as Ontario was concerned, the 1972 hostility toward Trudeau by the electorate seemed to have been switched to Stanfield. It may well have been because, in the lushness of Ontario's over-heated prosperity, the voters were angered by the Tory leader's appeal for economic restraint and controls. But it had to be something more than that, as Stanfield himself recognized. In his attempt to be a reasonable and responsible political leader, Stanfield found himself treated as a pariah.

It was a campaign a weaker man could not have endured. It is tribute to his courage that he never complained, even though he was sometimes atrociously treated by the press, nor did he waver in the course he had taken for himself. A demagogue might have done better, which is precisely what his critics are now suggesting. He could have made an issue of Quebec's language bill, and he could have swallowed the candidacy of Moncton's mayor, Leonard Jones. He could have cultivated the stock prejudices against Quebec and the underground hostility against federal policy in that province. He could have told the oilmen what they wanted to hear in Calgary.

That he did none of those things is not surprising to those who know him. Opportunism is as alien to him as is bigotry. Instead, he persisted in saying what he believed and nothing more.

The Ontario voters rejected not his policy but his leadership. Having now endorsed the leadership they wanted, we expect it will also be the leadership they deserve.

11 April 1977

What if, pray, the member for Crowfoot, Jack Horner, cannot be persuaded? Contrary to the unanimous opinion of the *Ottawa Citizen*, its editorial board, its pundits, and its shop steward in the printing plant — no, I do not think Jack Horner will defect to the Liberals.

My opinion is soundly based on reason and logic, which I hasten to add are mental processes that have doomed the careers of many a journalist. Notwithstanding, reason and logic do count for something, as I hope Jack Horner will shortly prove. My reasons he will not make the leap are surely cogent. First, Horner is a Conservative. Second, he is not a Liberal. Third, he is a man of stubborn principle, which is perhaps his most redeeming quality, and men of that kind are not likely to jettison their principles for a pass to the Liberal caucus, or a portfolio in a Liberal government, or a seat in the Liberal Senate.

There is some talk in the nation's capital that Horner is being used by the Liberals as an instrument to embarrass Joe Clark, the Tory leader, and, the argument runs, when it's all over, Horner will be in limbo, his credibility spent, and the Conservatives back to where they were — in a condition of internal turmoil. All this achieved by having Jack to lunch in the glowing company of James Coutts and Joyce Fairbairn, aides to the prime minister, followed by dinner at 24 Sussex Drive with P.E. Trudeau himself.

Other delights have been provided. A gushing editorial in the *Ottawa Citizen* has proclaimed the capture of Horner by the Liberals as a coup for "national unity" and described the member for Crowfoot as Parliament's leading authority on transportation and agriculture. The editorial concluded by dismissing Otto Lang from the cabinet and appointing Horner in his place.

If the conversion of Jack Horner could be consummated by stroking his ego, this past week spent in the Liberal body-rub parlour should more than do it. Not every one gets to dine at 24 Sussex — when was the last time Eugene Whelan was invited? — but then, a man like Horner is not to be proselytized by mere acolytes either.

Indeed, he would insist on meeting principals, in this case there being only one — the prime minister. Contrary to established opinion, it is my own that, in this bizarre episode, it is not Horner who is being used, but P.E. Trudeau. While the prime minister has taken pains to say that he offered nothing to Horner as alimony for his separation from the Tory caucus, Horner has let it be known that such a protestation is the kind of stuff they spread on the farm to make the grass greener. And in any test of credibility between these two, Jack wins hands down. So far.

To imagine that a man of Horner's stature, which is at least as great as his pride, would cross the floor merely to disappear in the back benches of the Liberal caucus is like suggesting a man would pack his things and leave New York City and move to Belfast to escape the muggings. No, there can be no doubt that Horner has an offer, which is more or less something like a platter with Otto Lang's head on it. Even less likely is the suggestion that the transmogrification of Jack Horner could be achieved by elevating him to the Senate, which would be little less than an act of subornation by the prime minister and of political suicide by Horner.

Still, it is a revelation that "national unity" — to return to the editorial previously noted — could be enhanced by ridding the Tory party of one of its most combative members. More revealing is the evidence that, as weak as the present Trudeau cabinet is deemed to be, there is nothing, or no one, on the back benches so worthy of consideration for promotion as Jack Horner, who sits on the other side of the House. Still more revealing is the tacit confession by Liberal strategists, including the prime minister, that the only way to win the West — in particular, Alberta — is not by winning seats through the electoral process but by winning over individual members of Parliament, which neatly bypasses the electoral system, so often untidy, and disenfranchises the voters by reversing their judgment and confounding their party preferences.

This exposé of the true nature and condition of present-day Liberalism we owe to Jack Horner. He has been taken up the mountain and shown the kingdom below, much of which could be his if he would only betray his innermost convictions. It is only fair to say that what has led him to this was not P.E. Trudeau, or Jim Coutts, or even Ms Fairbairn; Horner is mad as hell at Joe Clark, and frustrated by the fact that the boundaries of Crowfoot — the federal riding he has made a household word — have been all but obliterated by redistribution.

Still, one truly wonders whether Horner will live out his remaining days as the member for old Crowfoot, not as the familiar maverick, but as a turncoat Grit. Not, I think, for all the perks of power, a dozen limousines, or even Otto Lang's magic carpet. To exchange Crowfoot for Coventry, surely, is no exchange at all.

Being mad as hell at Joe Clark, whom Horner candidly dislikes, should not drive the Conservative member for Crowfoot into the embrace of the prime minister, whom he has never liked either. But what pique has failed to resolve ought now to be left to patience. There is running room in Alberta for Horner, if not in the tattered remainders of Crowfoot, then elsewhere. Of course, as a reconstituted Grit, Jack could run anywhere he liked, but not very far. His heart would not be in it, and many — too many — of his friends would be obliged to oppose him.

If Horner goes over to the Liberals, I will be the second most surprised man in the land, second only to Horner himself. He has not come this far by betraying his own gut reactions and we both know today what his visceral feelings are about his present dilemma.

22 April 1977

Extremely Confidential Memorandum to: J. Clark
From: W. Neville (aka "Intrepid")

To bring you up to date on Operation Trojan Horse, I wish to inform you, Chief, that Agent Horner swam ashore under cover of darkness and is now safely inside the walls. He entered the Kingdom through an open window in the parliamentary library (he had been provided with a map and directions by G. Fairweather) and, when the mission has been completed, he will leave through a side door of the Senate which has been left ajar.

Agent Horner is equipped with a two-way combination VHF short-wave radio, paper shredder, and stereo, five gallons of invisible ink, one year's supply of oatmeal cookies, and a do-it-yourself rye whiskey distilling kit. He is armed.

His instructions are to create maximum disruption in enemy communications; carry out specified acts of sabotage against the CNR; liquidate designated senior bureaucrats, ag. reps, French-language instructors, the CBC board of directors, and Otto Lang. He will also carry out harassment tactics calculated to confuse and undermine the PCO, the PMO, and the Canadian Wheat Board. For all these duties, as you know, Agent Horner has received special training.

Agent Horner's cover, as you suggested to the planning section, is that he is an undeveloped natural resource and has deserted us because he believes the war is lost and that he wants to bring peace to the Western Front. He is carrying on his person a counterfeit Liberal Party membership card (Crowfoot Chapter, membership No. 00001) and wearing cowboy boots with an AV-UHF-AM-FM transistorized tape recorder in the right heel. In the event anyone attempts to remove his boots, Agent Horner will self-destruct.

The strategic planning section of the special services branch, under my command, has instructed Agent Horner not to attempt to establish any contact with us while on this mission. As you yourself said to him, Chief, at the last briefing, "Don't call us, Jack. We'll call you."

According to reports from intelligence sources within the Kingdom, which are circulating inside the Alberta embassy, Agent Horner has already been offered the external affairs portfolio but has declined, telling the prime minister that he would settle for nothing less than a major post in the cabinet.

If I may be allowed a personal word or two, Chief, I recall the first time you proposed this mission for Agent Horner — it seems like only yesterday — and despite the early reservations expressed by the Contingency Assessment Board of the Strategic Planning Section of the Special Services Branch, and our wives, I am now glad to say we exerted all our energies to get this thing launched. Although we asked a great deal of Agent Horner, in terms of extreme personal discomfort and enormous risk, I could think of no one better equipped, in temperament and physical stamina, to undertake the mission, other than, say, Agent Schumacher, maybe.

The important thing, however, is that Agent Horner is now inside the walls and I am confident that within a short while he will be producing the desired results. We must all be patient, however, because we know that Rome was not built in a day, nor Troy levelled to the ground. Agent Horner needs time, and knowing your personal feelings about him, Chief, I know you will give him all the time in the world.

According to propaganda broadcasts from the Kingdom, picked up by our monitoring systems in the Monitoring Systems Branch of the Combined Operations Division (Terrorist Section), Agent Horner held a news conference at which he wept. As you probably know, Chief, this is a little trick we developed here especially for agents who are obliged to hold news conferences during a mission; all they do is put a wad of chewing tobacco under the tongue and swallow it when they get the first question. We suspect Agent Horner, when describing his feelings after deserting the cause, swallowed the whole plug.

Meanwhile, as per your instructions, we are working up plans for further missions, and despite the shortage of volunteers at this time, I am confident that one or two others may be found who might come forward and take the arduous training required in order to join Agent Horner. (Agent Cossitt comes to mind here.)

Anyway, Chief, so far, so good. The enemy have given no evidence whatsoever that they are aware of the operation and no doubt it will be some time before they know what hit them. And for all that, we owe a great deal to you for, in the first place, thinking up the idea, and, in the second place, finding the best man for the job.

If you wish to send any message to Agent Horner — and I doubt that you do — let me know. We have developed a number of ways of getting to Jack without breaking radio silence.

W. Neville (aka "Intrepid")

Chief-of-Staff, Special Services Branch.

8 February 1979

In one of Paul Hellyer's recent — um — syndicated effusions, I read the following: "The Tory party has no equal in its flair for self-immolation. No sooner does Joe Clark escape near-impalement on a soldier's bayonet, than his own troops start sniping from all directions."

Having established this somewhat tenuous battle-stations metaphor, wherein the author feels himself at home, the way is open to broader strokes of embellishment: "The first shot," Hellyer continues, "came from that master in the art of blood-letting, Dalton Camp. In a recent column, the éminence grise of leaders past and present blew the whistle on his national boss for. . ."

Well now, just hold on a minute.

For those of you who do not know who Paul Hellyer might be, or, indeed, for those who know only too well, a brief summary of his career might be in order.

I, for one, have stood in awe of his military record: as Liberal Minister of National Defence (circa 1963), he single-handedly did what numberless alien military leaders had failed to do in several wars, which was to sink the Royal Canadian Navy in the Sea of Integration, where it remains submerged to this day.

Having achieved the impossible, Hellyer next went into housing, and with much the same dedication as when he hurled himself upon Canada's armed forces. Indeed, it could be said that had Hellyer not been distracted from his mandate to resolve Canada's housing crisis of the sixties, we might all of us be living in caves today, in green uniforms.

Instead, Hellyer ran for the leadership of the Liberal Party — there being a vacancy — but unfortunately, for many of us, he did not win. Hellyer resigned from the Liberal Party and went off to form a party of his own, Action Canada, which he subsequently became the unanimous choice to lead.

Action Canada was, however, somewhat of a misnomer; as a party, it lacked a base and, as a movement, it lacked motion — its rate of progress having been measured at a speed roughly equal to that of the Athabaska glacier. This was not fast enough for Action Canada's leader, who resigned.

Paul Hellyer then did what any of us would surely have done, given all the circumstances. He joined the Conservative Party.

And lo — would you believe? — when a vacancy occurred for the leadership of that party, Hellyer once more offered himself. But, sure enough, what with one thing and another, including a nominating speech in which he frontally attacked some 30 per cent of those present and voting, Hellyer lost.

I mention these matters as gentle riposte to Hellyer's claim — "the Tory party has no equal in its flair for self-immolation." Given his own record, I think the author of that statement has the qualifications to instruct even the Tory party on the rites of self-immolation. In fact, were Hellyer to have a personal coat-of-arms — and who better — its escutcheon could be suitably emblazoned with a full can of gasoline and a lighted match.

Self-immolation has become an art with Mr. Hellyer, second only to his positive genius for scrambling metaphors, *exempli gratia*: "The first shot came from. . .Dalton Camp [who] blew the whistle." Later on, the shooting and whistling having subsided, Hellyer writes, "Camp draped his hatchet in a moral." (This is the prose, I take it, that dazed admirals of the fleet must have spent hours decoding, back in the good old days when Hellyer stood at the helm of our military juggernaut as it silently sailed into Mothball Harbour, N.S.)

But now, to the main point, which is this business of Dalton Camp blowing the whistle on "his national boss." I find the assertion breathtaking. Joe Clark is Dalton Camp's national boss? Or, put another way, my national boss is Joe Clark? How did all this come about? What are the hours? How about pension benefits? The Senate? Invitations to dinner at Sussex Drive? Pre-dynasty receptions at Stornoway? An introduction to Paul Hellyer?

I take from this only the morose conclusion that while columnist Hellyer knows who his boss is — Joe Clark — he only thinks he knows who mine is. He may also think Doug Fisher's national boss is Ed Broadbent, and that Stephen Lewis works for Michael Cassidy. Who does Charlie Lynch work for? Ed Schreyer?

Anyway, Paul, do me a favour. The next time you see your boss, give him my compliments. And tell him I just quit.

16 August 1979

We are all diminished by the passing of famous men — who stand taller than most of us; all of us are touched by it because the event reminds us, as little else does, of our own mortality. But of course the death of John Diefenbaker is of unique personal significance to me since it was my lot to be his eternal nemesis and adversary. Such has been the nature of our relationship for nearly fifteen years, which is longer than many friendships endure, and that it could remain so uncompromising and implacable for so long a time is perhaps an indication not only of the gulf of the misunderstanding and the lasting sense of grievance between us, but also that, even while it became increasingly irrelevant, our rivalry was worth keeping alive. If one must have foes in life, John Diefenbaker was one to be treasured. He may have thought the same of me.

I can well appreciate the curiosity of the media, as the phones attest now ringing with their enquiries at my home, cottage and office, inviting my comment on the news of his death. After all, to a considerable degree, our personal enmity was a creation of the media, which nourished it even unto this hour, and which gave it an endless continuity and enriched its texture. Certainly it kept it alive. That we were both foils to the uses of journalism must have occurred to him as it did to me, but there was, in the frequent, published exchange of barbs and shafts, many a coded message sent and received. It was the only way we had of keeping in touch.

But it should be understood, in light of the profound respect I held for our relationship, that I would not respond to this abrupt termination of it by muttering banalities and mindless platitudes. Nor would it be suitable to compose some obscenity of hypocrisy, meant as eulogy. I will leave that to others.

There were those who followed John Diefenbaker because they believed deeply in him, in what they deemed were his values and principles, and who detected in his exhortations the reaffirmation of a good many of their own beliefs. He was truly the only Canadian politician in our lifetime who had a personal constituency, one with an outlook and attitude close to his own. It must be said of him that he knew almost precisely who they were, and he never failed them. That constituency, of course, was not in Prince Albert alone, nor even in western Canada, but dispersed among numberless communities and neighbourhoods throughout the country — a private army wearing the armour of his righteousness, who never forsook his cause or forgave those who opposed it.

But they were never enough to sustain his leadership of either a government or a party. And while it would now be merely querulous to delineate the faults and failures which led to his fall from power, it needs to be remembered that the ultimate judgment of him as prime minister and as party leader was made by majorities of his fellow Canadians.

Perhaps they were wrong, a possibility which must be left to history's reappraisal, given that few of us are possessed of either hindsight or prescience. I suspect he will have a considerable place in the legends and lore of Canada, less as a successful politician but rather as a remarkable human being, whose force of personality and strength of character are without other example in our history and are likely to remain so.

His most memorable and endearing qualities were his most perverse: he was a man of considerable passion, but little forgiveness, and he was never plagued by honest doubts, as were so many of his contemporaries. He steered his course by the stubborn stars in a firmament of his own creation. Most of his admitted mistakes in politics, as his autobiography makes plain, and which read as trivial, were made under the duress of other opinions and against his own. He carried stubbornness beyond obduracy and made of it a personal virtue. Flexibility, like subtlety, was a vice. In argument or debate, he would never use a needle when a broad-axe would do. He took sustenance from conflict and encouragement from his opponents;

the more of them there were, the more certain he became that he was right.

It has been said of others, too often said of so many, that they were larger than life. That the observation has become trite is a pity: it should have been saved for John Diefenbaker. He had the qualities, flaws, foibles, and raw courage becoming only to figures of mythological proportions. The turbulent passage that was his life in politics cannot be assayed in the context of public policy or the national condition. It can only be weighed and measured in the nature and substance of the man.

Last, and finally, he was a man I once energetically supported and later vigorously opposed. If I was helpful to him as an ally or aide, I remained useful to him as the incarnation personified of his many adversaries. If this latter was occasionally irritating or discomfiting, I bore the burden of it with a stubborn pride worthy of him. He was an adversary of estimable mettle; I shall miss him, and in a way no other of his fellow Canadians would know.

6 December 1979

At the same moment P.E. Trudeau was announcing his resignation as Liberal leader at an Ottawa news conference, I was in the very midst of explaining to an enthralled audience on the set of "Take Thirty" (a TV show out of Toronto) that the political future of the same P.E. Trudeau was not as bleak as many believed.

Indeed, I was in the process of speaking of the possibility that he might well come storming back to power, given a turnabout in the public's opinion of him in the province of Ontario, when the floor director in the studio shouted "Stop Tape!" and we were then advised that the Liberal leader had just turned in his mantle. It became a story I told on myself and one which later found its way into a newspaper column, bearing the moral that a pundit's life can be a hard one.

But not all that hard, I can now say, having read the latest Gallup Poll, which serves as the litmus test of a pundit's worth in between elections and other man-made disasters. According to Gallup, Trudeau's approval rating, among those sampled, is now more than three times higher than that of C.J. Clark, the incumbent prime minister, while the Liberal Party has lengthened its lead over the Conservatives — the bulge created largely by a turnabout in public opinion in Ontario.

Well, a pundit I may be, but a mind-reader I ain't. Had the Liberal leader consulted me, I could have warned him of the grave possibility of a resurrection in his popularity — namely in Ontario —

and had he held back his resignation until after this recent poll, he might have been physically restrained from resigning by assorted aides and actuaries. At the very least — since the poll was conducted before the announcement of his quitting — Trudeau would have been spared reading all those stories about his resignation being hastened by the soulful conclusion that he was finished as a politician.

What I keep reminding the students in my class on Elementary Politics is that a politician is never dead so long as he is still walking around. I considered Trudeau as likely a deposed leader as any of historic example of being able to renew his lease on power, given some luck and a little help from his friends, the Tories. All he would need to do would be to hold fast to his base in Quebec and restore his support in Ontario, never mind what providential bonus seats might fall to him in the far west or east.

Whether Trudeau jumped or fell from his perch, he leaves behind him the intriguing possibility that, had he hung on, he might have made Mackenzie King's tenure as prime minister look like a mere inter-regnum.

Still, if he had to go, for whatever reasons, he went out at a time when it could be said of him that he was close to recapturing a good part of his old constituency.

But one needs to do more than read the numbers: one needs to ask, "How come?" Fair to say, I think, that Trudeau was, and is, less than a thundering success as an opposition leader. Apart from that, what can be remembered of him, after the fall, is that he retrieved his vintage Mercedes, resumed his habit as world traveller, went canoeing, grew a beard, and eschewed a gathering of British Columbia Liberals for the opportunity to disco in New York. That any or all of these would prove so endearing to the masses is a puzzle. Perhaps, instead, we should look elsewhere for clues to this phenomenon of the high standing of P.E. Trudeau in the hearts of his countrymen in most parts of the country.

Something tells me all this has less to do with Trudeau than with his replacement, prime minister Clark. Perhaps it is not that the people who were polled like Trudeau more these days but that they like Clark less. Having recently made a sweep of the country, from east to west and to Ottawa, I can report hearing no one out there singing the praises of the Tory leader. If the new government were a play just opened on Broadway, it would be shut down tomorrow for bad reviews.

From my seat in the house, I think it's a bad rap. If the first act has been uneven, and the second a drag, I'm yet prepared to await the next few scenes before leaving the theatre. But the awful truth is that the great unseen audience seems to be afflicted by a terminal, total indifference, which is a state well in advance of boredom and ennui.

For reasons as yet unfathomed, too many Canadians know little or nothing about Clark and, more important, would just as soon not be told. Perhaps the man who campaigned so determinedly as an ordinary fellow from the foothills has managed to convince everyone of his ordinariness. Having done so, not even the office of prime minister improves the self-imposed image of an ordinary man capable only of average performance, a fellow who is too much like the rest of us. So while the country has been going about rediscovering P.E. Trudeau — which has proved a waste of its time — the next puzzle is when it will go about discovering C.J. Clark, if ever.

22 March 1980

It seems to me that federal labour minister Gerald Regan has had a bad rap from the media, if not from the RCMP, whose little document it was which contained the unremarkable information that, as provincial party leader, Regan's income was supplemented by payments from a party trust fund. The media treatment given the divulged document has done some damage to Regan's reputation and further political aspirations, and that seems to me to be manifestly unfortunate, unnecessary and unfair.

In reporting all this, a headline on the front page of one daily newspaper reads: "Regan Accepted Money." Alongside is a two-column picture of the minister of labour, looking suitably uncomfortable, while the caption beneath begins with the words: "Subject of Investigation."

The trouble with the headline is not that it's false — Regan *did* accept money — but the pejorative ring of it, which conjures in the reader's mind the numberless possibilities by which a politician would "accept money" when he shouldn't. It would be as though the headline had read: "Regan Took Bath," which could only suggest to the average reader that such would be news because Regan needed one.

As for the caption, the only trouble with that, so far as I know, is that it's untrue — that Regan "accepted money" from a party trust fund is not the subject of a police investigation. Were it so, it would be news to Regan, who says he has never been contacted by the RCMP on the matter.

It is remarkable how such a common practice — that of political parties supplementing the incomes of their leaders (as well as others) — can be made to seem sinister and, indeed, to reflect upon the integrity of the beneficiaries. In this latest example, Gerald Regan has been the victim, largely because of the irrelevant fact that the information on his additional income comes from a police dossier, flushed out into public light as the result of a court order, and because it was also associated with a police investigation into party fund-raising practices.

Regan could be said to have suffered an accident to his reputation. Some would even say it was unavoidable, since it has become the fashion to impute motives and wrong-doing to politicians simply because they are in politics. There is a pervasive belief that politics is awash with venality and corruption and, therefore, since politicians must be up to something at least some of the time, they must be assumed to be guilty until they have occasion to prove their innocence. Unhappily, even when they do, the memory of the imputation survives long past their exoneration.

What we ask of people in public life is that they allow themselves to be defamed in the presumed public interest, which is to say the presumption of their dishonesty is regarded as the safest way to ensure their honesty. Such a doctrine has led us into the abomination of conflict of interest "guidelines," which will do more to discourage people of quality from entering politics and to encourage titillation and public voyeurism than they will ever do to safeguard the system.

The Regan *affaire* prompts me to express a concern I have had for some time. The RCMP has been conducting what appears to be an endless enquiry, on a national scale, into the methods and practices of political fund-raising. Some of the "news" of the enquiry — portions of which have been mysteriously leaked to the media and to selected politicians — has been lurid enough to excite public curiosity, loaded up, as it is, with such buzz-words as "kick-backs" and "toll-gates." Thus far, the investigation has done more to degrade the political system even further in the public mind and injure the reputation of innocent participants in the system — the example of Regan being only the latest — than to demonstrate any measure of legitimacy for what has been, in fact, an extensive fishing trip.

What has struck me about the mission of the RCMP is an apparent zealousness that approaches frenzy to "get their man," even when he may not exist. To be charitable, what has characterized the performance of the police so far has been their limitless capacity for suspicion, which has only been equalled by their ignorance of the system they are investigating.

15 June 1980

Well now, wait a minute. A man who sometimes races cars for a living, name of Maurice Carter, and who twice ran as a Tory candidate — unsuccessfully — in an Ontario provincial election, is being stoned in the streets, and in the Ontario legislature, for saying, allegedly, that he has hated Germans ever since he landed in Europe in World War II.

The subject is somewhat complicated because Carter made the statement (although quoted "out of context," according to a designated spokesman) while alighting on German soil as the driver of a racing car in which the government of Ontario holds a $15,000 interest. The racing car is scheduled to compete at Le Mans, wherever that is, even as you are reading this; indeed, the race may already be over.

But not the frothing of politicians, who need nothing more to gird themselves in the corsets of virtue than a numb, indiscreet clanger such as that dropped by Carter. A New Democrat — in truth, the same who defeated Carter at the polls and who should have been, ever after, grateful — has described Ontario's newest wheelie as "a Tory hack and a self-admitted bigot." The government of Ontario has assumed various supine positions, apologizing for their racing driver's mouth (although he still gets to keep the car).

Let's see now. The hon. member who referred to Carter as a "Tory hack" must have had in mind that the subject of his asseveration became a hack by opposing him in an election. Which suggests a paraphrase of an old joke: murder your wife and you'll be known as a man once provoked by ungovernable passion; people will line up to have you for dinner. Run once against the NDP and you're a Tory hack for the rest of your life.

On the other hand, had not Carter had the inexplicable clumsiness to lose to the NDP, and were he not provincially subsidized in his even more inexplicable urge to race at Le Mans, his attitude towards the Germans would be a matter of some considerable indifference.

As of now, I have not given much thought — although obviously as much as anyone else — about the rectitude of the Ontario government's position. I mean, should the Ontario government fund an Ontario-assembled car, driven by a Tory hack, to race at Le Mans? Should it do so, were the driver a Liberal hack? Or, say, even were the driver a noble, virtuous, upright pillar of society, such as a defeated candidate for the NDP (which would allow for a more discerning choice among a limitless supply)?

Certainly it cannot be said that governments are beneath subsidizing heavens-knows-who-or-what to go overseas and excel, or come second, or to show, as a means of improving upon the world's awareness of, for example, Canada, Quebec, Ontario, or their exports. Governments do it all the time. Do you think our glorious Canadian hockey teams travel abroad, pounding Swedes against the boards, at their own expense?

Burrowing further into this heap of sanctimony, we come to Larry Grossman, the Ontario minister who stands in direct line of fire, since it was he who sent racing driver Carter on his way with envelope in hand containing the fifteen grand, and O-N-T-A-R-I-O painted on the fender of his machine.

Grossman could be at fault here. Before handing over the money, he should have interrogated Carter.

"Maurice, old hack," he might have asked. "Before you leave, how do you feel about Germans, since you last landed in Europe in World War II?"

And Maurice Carter, were he any sort of racing driver at all, would have replied, "Well, Larry, I guess I feel the same way about them as you do."

At this writing, the politicians, and the hacks, are running for cover. There are not enough mea culpas to go round.

But the truth is harder than that. No, sir, generations of Canadians have not forgiven Germany for its barbarism, and a large number of those who fought against it never will. I happen to remember how men like Carter were imbued with that hatred, which was not without its legitimacy in the horrors known then and found since. Unlike Carter, most of those who survived that experience have kept their lips buttoned. But not even a politician should be dumb enough to pretend it has been forgotten — or forgiven.

One would hesitate to award racing driver Carter points for diplomacy. He is an unlikely candidate for appointment to another Ontario trade mission to Germany, and it would be happier for all concerned if, from now on, he allowed his car to do the talking, and put the muffler in his mouth.

Still, if what the man said constitutes prima facie bigotry, then he represents a whole generation of bigots who were zealously trained, indoctrinated, and indeed paid, to hate. That the sentiment has endured so long in some is not necessarily the sign of defective character but a somewhat embarrassing tribute to the residual effects of a nation's success in preparing its youth for slaughter in a cause deemed to be the ultimate in worthiness. While it is discomfiting to be reminded of all this, it is more painful to listen to the bleats of politicians who apparently have nothing to forget.

11 July 1980

A political science professor from British Columbia, writing in one of Canada's national newspapers (the other being *La Presse*), seems to be saying, as I gleaned from the headline over his article, that our political

33

parties have become defunct. They are no longer vital, relevant, or much fun either.

Since I have been saying so myself often over the past five years — indeed, with such regularity that I eventually discarded it as a topic even for chattering up cocktail parties in Mississauga — my curiosity is piqued as to how news of the decline of the political parties ultimately crossed the Canadian Rockies and penetrated the academic mists which apparently permanently engulf the political science department at the University of British Columbia.

That the obvious dawns so late in Vancouver could be put down to the movement of the sun, from east to west in most places, or ascribed to the phenomenon of western alienation, a term employed by western politicians as response to the inscrutable mysteries of federal policy for transportation, communications, energy, agriculture, the fishery, and Senate reform.

But yes, it's true that political parties are not what they used to be, and have not been for some time. While this is palpably evident, as witness the recent Liberal Party gathering in Winnipeg, there is irony in the fact that the parties are nonetheless more affluent than they have ever been, and have the power to dismiss their leaders, even one who is a prime minister — clout they have had only in recent years.

Given this, the Liberal Party as seen last week in Winnipeg, or the Tory party when seen in Ottawa next winter, bears little resemblance to the gathering of the formidable elites in past years. More and more they look less and less like people of status, stature and influence who once shaped their parties and, through them, the country itself.

Averageness dominates the scene: no one, with the conspicuous exception of the prime minister, rises above the crowd. No one emerges from it but everyone recedes into it. Too many of those present, of course, have become household words — such as Munro, Pepin, Whelan, Drāno, Jello and Rinso. None of this is so distressing as the awareness that there doesn't appear to be anyone else; not since 1968 — imagine — has there been an injection of new blood in the Liberal Party.

The party system no longer produces a credible crop of potential leaders. How could one rise in today's political party if one is obliged only to be mute and otherwise agreeable? The trick nowadays is not to develop talent but to repel it.

But the real killers of political parties have been money and television. Money buys expertise, which debases the value of voluntarism; money pays for public opinion polls and nullifies the role of the grassroots as a source for political intelligence; and money buys television, which allows the politicians and their hired hands direct access to the electorate, for which neither the party's involvement nor its advice need be solicited.

So, you might ask, pray then what were those folk doing in Winnipeg? Well, many of them were seeing more of the country. Others were relieving the tedium of their lives, fighting inflation and all that drear, with a painless immersion in communal liturgy. A few might have smuggled into the meeting place some small private ambition, such as a seat in the Senate, or a slot on the tariff board. But who knows?

What they weren't doing there was drafting new policy, setting a new course, or building a better Canada. Not that Liberal delegates necessarily ever did any of these things, but it used to be they always thought they did. There have even been times when you could say they just about did. Not, however, this time or the last time, or next time.

What we don't know is where this will lead us. Obviously, political power now flourishes outside the party system, concentrated among a few insiders, so few as to count them upon the fingers of one hand — maybe two hands if you also count deputy ministers. And the slogan for the Liberals meeting in Winnipeg was, "The future is now." If that was the future we saw, they can keep it.

31 September 1980

One of the toughest questions on Canadian politics is also one that's often asked — possibly because no one has ever given a satisfactory answer. The question is: "What's the difference between the Liberals and the Conservatives anyway?"

As a service to students of political science, and other readers, I propose to answer the question. So pay attention back there.

The real difference between a Conservative and a Liberal these days is that a Tory believes in the Deity and a Grit believes in Advertising. This is not to say a Liberal is, by definition, an agnostic; Liberals believe in a Supreme Being, but where their ideology and their theology come together is in their unshakable faith in the Power of Advertising — in that Unholy Trinity of the Pollster, the Copywriter and the One-Minute Commercial.

Conservatives also believe in Advertising, but only a little. Religion matters more to Tories because so much has happened to them, especially lately, that defies explanation. Tories best explain it by believing Someone up there knows what He's doing, even though they

35

don't. But if you ask a Conservative to renew the Canadian constitution, he'll call a conference; if you ask a Liberal, he'll call his advertising agency.

This perfect truth was impressed on me when I read of the pilgrimage to New York City, the mecca of Advertising, made by Martin Goldfarb, pollster; Jerry Grafstein, president of the Liberal in-house ad agency; Terry O'Malley, president of a Liberal out-house ad agency; Norman MacLeod, president of the Liberal Party, and Senator Keith Davey, well-known prestidigitator and rainmaker.

These gentlemen went together to the Big Apple to appear before a group of — you've guessed it — New York advertising executives, to offer testimony as to their profound faith, based on personal experience, in the Supreme Power of Advertising, yesterday, today, and forever and ever, Amen.

Speaking of their salvation, Goldfarb and Davey told how the miraculous powers of Advertising restored P.E. Trudeau to office and themselves to more comfortable quarters adjacent. The miracle produced the successful result in the 1980 Canadian federal election campaign in which they played, of course, vital roles. And while few of their listeners quite knew where Canada was located, other than nearby, all of the New York advertising executives were impressed. Indeed, so raptly attentive was the audience that the only sound to be heard in the room was of the Canadian ad men scratching their own backs.

Goldfarb is a man who, if Advertising were instead the Church, would be at least a Cardinal. He told the New York ad execs that the single issue in the campaign of 1980 was "fear." The voters, he said, were afraid of Joe Clark. This does not explain the fearless voters of Saskatchewan, Alberta and British Columbia, who cast their ballots for anything that moved provided it was not a Grit. But I can refine Goldfarb's hypothesis for him: in that part of the country, the voters were terrified of Trudeau, and still are. Goldfarb also becomes the first prophet of the Advertising Age to tell us that the voters of Quebec, who made the difference in that campaign between Liberal victory or defeat, voted so overwhelmingly for Trudeau because Joe Clark scared them stiff. It is, however, a thought unique for its novelty, if not for its profundity.

Senator Keith Davey's contribution to improved international understanding and strengthened faith in Advertising came on the heels of his explanation of how Liberal campaign strategy was developed to hide Trudeau from the voters, lest they forget their fear of Clark and remember their fear of *him*. The senator described his leader, with characteristic understatement, as "the most charismatic leader in

Canadian history," ignoring, I thought, the just claims of past charismatic leaders, such as J.J. Abbott and Mackenzie Bowell. Still, hyperbole begs the question: How come "the most charismatic leader in Canadian history" had to be hidden from view for the entire campaign? The answer must be: if you have charisma, you shouldn't let on.

The Madison Avenue ad execs might have asked: if the Liberal advertising campaign was such a success, how come the Grits blew half of their twenty-point lead in the polls during the campaign? But no one asked. You don't get to Heaven by asking dumb questions of True Believers.

10 October 1980

Joe Clark came last week to the Tory sanctorum of the Albany Club, located in the canyons of Mammon in downtown Toronto. The federal leader was there to speak on his party's determination to resist the proposed package for constitutional change now before Parliament in the name of the Liberal government of P.E. Trudeau. Seated above the salt and beside him was Bill Davis, the premier of Ontario, who had only a week before urged members of Parliament, including those in Clark's caucus, to support the Trudeau proposals.

Also present were MPs Allan Lawrence and Mike Wilson, along with Bill Neville, Clark's chief policy advisor, and Bill Saunderson, commandant to the federal Ontario organization, among others. And of course, deployed throughout the house were representatives of Ontario's provincial organization, the Big Blue Machine, including the Albany Club's president, Norman Atkins. As well, there was the spectral presence of Sir John A. Macdonald, the Albany's founding father, who ninety-nine years ago became its first charter member so that he could have a suitable place in Hogtown for libation and other sustenance. Sir John builded better than he knew.

By longstanding custom, these ritual dinners are private affairs and off the record, the Albany not yet being vulnerable to the Freedom of Information Act. But it can be reported, without betraying the tradition of non-disclosure, that anyone who came to dine on confrontation or recrimination between Clark and Davis went away hungry. The benign presence of the premier, called upon to thank the speaker, was a part of the evening's diffusion, and Clark's muted speech, which some of his listeners suspected was not entirely the one he had come prepared to make, was another. The message from both, to the members inside, the media outside, and the multitudes beyond, was that their disagreement, however profound, was impersonal and, indeed, mutually understood to be irreconcilable. It is a message which Metternich, Bismarck, Machiavelli, and even Sir John would have understood — there's no politics like realpolitik.

At the heart of the matter is an emergent reality in Canadian politics. The true political base of the federal Tory party is no longer in Ontario, but in the West. Western Canada has become, for the Tories, what Quebec has been for the Liberals — a very nearly impregnable bastion of support. And while history has produced Liberals for generations from the cradles of Quebec, it will likely do the same for federal Conservatives in the four western provinces for some time to come.

The new coin of the realm is energy — oil and gas — and the divisions within the country are between those who have it and those who don't. Appeals to the national interest or party loyalty are not enough to bridge the gap where self-interest has created polarity. It allows few politicians much choice and Joe Clark and Bill Davis none at all. Any Tory federal leader who stood with Trudeau and against the provincial governments of British Columbia, Alberta, Saskatchewan, Manitoba, Nova Scotia and Newfoundland would be reappraised on the spot.

As for the only two provincial premiers who support the federal constitutional proposals, Ontario's Bill Davis and New Brunswick's Richard Hatfield, it is more than coincidence that neither of them has a barrel of oil or a cubic foot of natural gas to his name. Much of the media analysis which has attended this Clark-Davis confrontation has been, to say the least, frivolous. The CBC, as though it had been feasting on magic mushrooms, treated the conflict among the Tories as a re-enactment of the Diefenbaker saga, or by conjecturing that Davis was out to get Clark's job. (If true, the Liberals would be pleased to send money.)

A more relevant observation might be that the politics of Canada are being restructured, and the reconfiguration of the federal Conservative Party is only a part of the process. Ontario's dominant place in the federal Tory party, enough to give it veto power over policy, and first call upon the decisions of its leaders, is plainly at an end. What one does, as a politician, when the inevitable becomes obvious, is to do as Davis and Clark did at the Albany Club: forsake your differences and save your breath to cool your soup.

Up in York North, the only Toronto federal constituency where folks regularly ride to hounds, a Tory committee is conducting "an open, yet restrained, campaign" to unseat its federal leader, Joe Clark. The dissident committee is not, it says, sending out press releases, looking for interviews, or going to the media in search of publicity. No sir. The reason I know this is true is because I read it in the committee's own newspaper, which is circulated to any and all who have an address and good relations with the post office.

The paper is called the *PC Review News*, which puts it right up there with the *Antigonish Casket* for owning a no-nonsense name. The *Review News* is not only printed on nice stock with an extra colour — blue — but it also has a philosophy and a goal. Not to keep you in suspense, its goal is "the re-establishment of the Progressive Party as the governing Party of Canada." (I know, I know — but that's what it says, and John Bracken would have loved it.)

In the paper's Statement of Philosophy, we read: "The lifeblood of these ten provinces and two territories, joined together in a nation, is dependant upon we as Progressive Conservatives being successful." Us won't argue that, grammar being no more elusive to the editors of *Review News* than syntax. (As example: "We must as a Party put forth policies, ideals, and visions for the future that will excite Canadians from sea to sea to join with us as John Diefenbaker did.")

Speaking of exciting visions, the Review Committee has one of its own: "Canada," it says, "is fast sinking in a divided sea."

On the second page of the *Review News*, we read that the committee "is definitely *not* conducting a dump the leader campaign." On the third page, the paper reprints four articles about Joe Clark taken from various newspapers — "honest expressions by concerned journalists," it calls them — each of which calls for Clark to quit. In journalism, we call that balanced reporting.

But if the Tory committee is not out to nail Clark, its own Member of Parliament, John Gamble, apparently is. Gamble is something of an original thinker, and his thoughts, as expressed under his byline in the *Review News*, will be news to everyone, including Clark.

"It was largely through his efforts," Gamble writes of his leader, "that our constitution now provides for the automatic, secret ballot question on a leadership convention."

The only thing wrong with that, of course, is that it's completely false. But it would be a mistake not to read into Gamble's version of recent history in "this great Party of Macdonald and Diefenbaker among others," anything other than a profound ignorance or an active malice.

"We must not go fishing for votes in a pond but mount a tidal wave of support," Gamble writes, awash in a sea of metaphor. Explaining how he came to join the movement launched by his own executive ("I found those supporters and they became. . . the officers of our riding executive"), Gamble offers as compelling reason. "One of the most convincing arguments presented to me was that our Party required the mass media exposure that comes with a leadership convention. Statistically the public perception of a political party improves immediately after a leadership convention."

I have been told that Gamble's committee asked the Tory party's national office to provide it with lists of party supporters so that more Tories could read *Review News*. I'm also told the national office turned down the request.

It was a mistake. If Joe Clark really wants to keep his job, he should give Gamble's supporters all the lists he can lay his hands on.

11 November 1980

As you probably know by now, I am a resolutely lukewarm supporter of the prime minister's patriation package, an enthusiasm for it appropriate to one who would as soon the subject had never come up. But as I keep saying to those who would settle for patriation only, or patriation with the entrenchment of rights and an amending formula, or an amending formula without entrenchment, or for putting the whole thing off until some other time — look, I keep saying, have you ever considered the absolutely staggering benefits and unqualified blessings to follow, once we get this over with?

Like what, you ask.

Take the first and most obvious. Once we have brought the constitution to Canada, we can forget about it. Having been out of sight and mind for the better part of 113 years over in London, it can as easily be forgotten in Ottawa. Our federal government may then turn to drawing up a new agenda, comprising the many presently unattended and unresolved problems of Canada — possibly even one or two of your own.

Furthermore, when this long ordeal is over, and patriation becomes a fact, the prime minister will retire, still a winner, and with a snug niche in Canadian history. (You've heard of The Great Emancipator? Move over, Abe, here comes The Great Patriator.) For many Canadians of all faiths, including Liberals, the peaceful retirement of P.E. Trudeau is a consummation devoutly to be wished; those now hurling themselves against the barricades are only postponing the day of their own deliverance.

Imagine, the combined delights of a new national agenda and a new national leader — enough fresh energy released into the political atmosphere to jolt the economy into second gear. Yet this is no more than the prime minister has promised. Give him his way, and he'll go away. Our trouble is that, as long as we've known him, we still can't read his signals.

Only the other day, at his media conference, he did everything but stand on his chair and wave his arms. He saw no reason, he said, why the constitutional package couldn't arrive in Canada from Westminster as early as April. His message ought to have been clear: he dreads the thought of another summer in Ottawa and is prepared to waive the little ceremony planned for July 1st (at which time we were to celebrate our final release from the shackles of colonialism) if only his opposition will cooperate in arranging for his early retirement. I think that's an offer we would be unwise to refuse.

As though these are not enticements enough to make converts out of obstructionists, there are more delights to come, in the post-patriation politics of Canada. To name one, John Turner.

At the Tory leadership convention in 1967, one of the candidates, Donald Fleming, campaigned on the slogan, "Donald Fleming is ready now." It did not turn out to be a winner, but a fellow with Turner's credentials, history and pure luck just happens to be the readiest politician in Canada.

You have only to submit yourself to the briefest interrogation to be convinced that the Liberal Party, become specialists in resurrections, will soon be embarked on the Turner Restoration. Indeed, a coronation is at hand.

But first, the quiz:

"What card-carrying member of the federal Liberal Party can you name who still gets invitations (and accepts) to speak in places like Vancouver, Calgary, Regina and Winnipeg?"

"What anglophone Liberal do you know who is fluently bilingual and has held senior portfolios in the federal government?"

"What card-carrying Liberal could you name who has (a) relatives in British Columbia, (b) a job in Toronto, (c) held a seat in Parliament from Quebec, (d) lived in Rockcliffe, and (e) been a good friend of Keith Davey's?"

"Name a ranking Liberal politician who bears no responsibility whatever for (a) 1980 Liberal election promises, (b) Allan MacEachen's budget, (c) patriating the constitution, and, (d) getting on Peter Lougheed's nerves."

Then, a final question. "At present there are believed to be at least twelve leadership aspirants in the Liberal caucus. Name one."

John Turner is ready now. Those of you filibustering against patriation are simply wasting your time. And his.

The Canadian taxpayer pays $100 million a year to graze 282 hon. members of the House of Commons on Parliament Hill. This sum includes the cost of feed, keeping their hair short, salaries for researchers to tell them what the facts are, and speechwriters to tell them what to say about what the facts are, plus secretaries to type letters to be delivered postage-free to constituents, telling them how great a job hon. members are doing keeping down the cost of government.

What this means is that it now costs $354,000 a year just to service one Member of Parliament. None of that amount includes the member's salary, tax-free allowance, indexed pension, and other invisibles such as free travel. The auditor general, who conducted an examination into how the nation's watchdogs of the Treasury conduct themselves in their own kennel, turned in a scathing report to Madame Speaker Sauvé and then, understandably, retired from office. As a man who has spent a good part of his life tracking down waste, extravagance and boondoggling in government, he can now tell his grandchildren he has seen it all.

A short answer to the question as to how this country has become nearly ungovernable is that the governors are unable to govern themselves. Doug Fisher, who served time in Parliament and writes about it with authority, often insisted that the basic role of the MP was to scrutinize the government's spending estimates. If they would even do that these days, they would do us all a great service. And as a first step, hon. members should begin by examining their own spending. As matters stand, there could not be enough gall, even in a Member of Parliament, to allow one of them to accuse the government of over-spending, or empire-building, or otherwise submitting the taxpayer to cruel and inhuman punishment — not, that is, and keep a straight face while doing so.

That much, of course, is obvious. What is less so has been the drift away from the traditional model of the parliamentarian as a generalist in the public's service, into a more recent one of man-child in never-never land. It is hard to know what MPs do for a living these days. We do know, whatever it is, it takes more time to do it, and more people to do it for them. There are three thousand hired helpers on

Parliament Hill, all of them employed to make the life of an MP bearable. Somewhere in that swarm of humanity, one could doubtless discover the man who ghosted the first speech about cutting government spending by reducing the numbers employed in the government bureaucracy.

There has been, in recent years, an effort to make the House of Commons a parallel power of government, to provide Members of Parliament with comparable resources in research and other ancillary services to those enjoyed by the ministry.

Since most ministerial statements are prepared by someone else, it then follows that most of the speeches made by members should be written by someone else. And since the answers to questions raised in the House are prepared by someone else, it follows that the questions themselves ought to be prepared by someone else. And so it goes. The true contest in Parliament is now become one between two bureaucracies, that of the ministry and the other on the Hill; the elected members have become merely their mouthpieces. It does no good to argue, as has been done, that there is no practical or possible way by which the private member can compete with the government in research, hard information and raw intelligence. You can always try; but even for $100 million you still won't come close.

9 December 1980

Those who have been complaining of inflation and the high cost of survival will be inspired by the solution discovered by their Members of Parliament. It's quite simple: pay yourself more money. It's a solution that's been lying around all this while right under their noses in Ottawa, where senior civil servants have had their salaries increased by 50 percent over the past six years. So, if you find yourself running out of money while standing at the check-out counter in the supermarket, stop whimpering and get on with it. Raise your own pay.

The way it will work for the MPs is on the principle of creeping escalation: today, they draw down a salary of $30,000, four years later it becomes $55,000, nudged along by an annual raise of $3,500, plus a further adjustment for whatever the cost of living increase struck at the beginning of each year. Additionally, hon. members will have up to a $6,000 tax-free allowance for housekeeping expenses in Ottawa, plus $7,500 tax-free for out-of-pocket expenses.

Never let it be said the folks in Ottawa talk about inflation but never do anything about it. Indeed, there can't be much reason for anyone to talk about inflation any longer. The problem's solved; Ottawa is now wall-to-wall inflation-proof.

43

Some of us, of course, will be left out in the cold, noses pressed against the window, looking in upon this parliamentary Feast of Stephen. Nor would we blame hon. members, much less begrudge them their good fortune, because, you see, this new money has been thrust upon them. The revised salary scale is the recommendation of a commission of two former MPs which has just made hon. members an offer they can't refuse.

One of the commissioners, Leon Balcer, told a news conference that he'd met a lot of able people who would dearly love to be Members of Parliament but who were repelled by the low pay and "the uncertainties of politics." But what uncertainties? Assuredly not those of tenure. Liberal members from Quebec or Tory ones from Alberta, for example, are more likely to be struck by lightning than lose their seats. It has been proven by recent example that the only way a Tory can be defeated in Alberta is for him to accept a cabinet post in a Liberal government; and proven to the point of absurdity that all that's necessary for a lifetime career in Parliament is a Liberal nomination in Quebec.

The commissioner also described the beneficiaries of his study — the hon. members — as underpaid and overworked. This does not explain how it is that hon. members beg to be re-elected every time the writs are issued, or why, over the past quarter-of-a-century, only four members come to mind (John Hamilton, Robert Mitchell, Doug Fisher, John Reynolds) who quit because of the working conditions.

Unquestionably, hon. members are entitled to a salary increase and to adjustments in their perquisites. What the commissioners have proposed, however, is excessive and guaranteed to hasten and harden the demands of everyone else in the country upon a floundering economy.

We are continually hearing the admonitory cries for restraint from precisely the same people who have been unable to restrain themselves, as witness the report of the auditor general. It is becoming difficult to maintain the illusion that the role of the parliamentarian is one of public service when, in the midst of a period of economic distress, Members of Parliament indemnify themselves from inflation simply by paying their way out of it.

Mr. Balcer's homilies aside, we do not elect the best available people to public office but, instead, we elect ordinary mortals — God knows — who are more or less like ourselves. And we do not elect them to some distant remote, nor reward them so they may be oblivious to our concerns. The reality today is that inflation is hurting almost everyone; there is no reason why our politicians should not also feel a little of the pain.

Finally, another of the commission's proposals ought to be implemented only after the millennium. It recommends that constituents be allowed to call their MP toll-free — not so much a hot-line as a whine-line. If installed, what follows, as night follows day, is a vast army of new employees on Parliament Hill raised and paid to answer the phones; and another army to answer the questions received on answering the phones. And then more to answer the phone from callers answering the answers to their previous call. Before we know it, $55,000 a year won't be enough to pay them for answering all those phones.

12 December 1980

You cannot argue with stupidity, someone said, you can only pity it. And one can only pity the mental squalor of those few Tories in Parliament who shouted down a motion moved by the NDP member for Regina East to mark the death of John Lennon, gunned down outside his New York apartment building. The caterwaulers who denied the mover's request for unanimous consent were led by John Gamble MP, audibly become Head Dinosaur of the Neanderthal wing in the federal Tory caucus.

The singular fact of this matter, the nub of its unseemliness, is that the nay-sayers had no real perception of who John Lennon was, had never truly heard his music, nor listened to his words, nor could have been even dimly aware of the man's profound influence upon a generation of the world's young. The NDP member's motion, they decided instantly, was "not a matter of national importance."

They were right — they always are, in a bizarre way. It was not a matter of national importance, but merely global; Lennon's death evoked tribute to his work and stature from just about everyone from Ronald Reagan to Mick Jagger, representing a political spectrum approaching infinity.

A trouble with ignorance is that it is so often intolerant; the problem with political yahoos is that they are an embarrassment to the occupation of politician. And I suppose some of us are doomed forever, as members of a lost tribe of conservatives, to be continually mortified by a Conservative party which has made yahooism central to its dogma.

Right about here, I should admit to a considerable lack of authority as a judge of the work of John Lennon, the Beatles, and Yoko Ono. Indeed, they did not make my favourite music. And, truer still, there must have been more than a little self-serving among the outpouring of tribute to Lennon — in his own words, "Everybody loves you when you're six feet in the ground" — but one would be a fool not to recognize the man's hold on millions, for whom his songs were metaphor for their stubborn idealism. That he was, like them, often confused, tormented and flouting of convention remains irrelevant to the clarity

45

and integrity of feeling in his poetry. Genius comes in many disguises, but not all the chaos, clatter and celebrity which surrounded Lennon's career could conceal the impact and force of his message, or diminish a talent that was an altogether unique gift. All one needed to recognize it was an ear to listen and, I suppose, some acquaintance with the real world.

Given the state of politics, it would be unreasonable to assume that all hon. members under the roof of the National Gas Works would comprehend the importance of John Lennon. Politicians, to begin with, could easily resent any man with so baffling a talent and so huge a constituency. That so many of the young and not-so-young understood Lennon while never understanding politicians would not only be puzzling but irritating. Besides, there was the — well — lifestyle: the hair, the granny glasses, the pot, and the menacing uniforms of the anti-establishment.

Doubtless, then, some felt threatened by what they did not understand. But ignorance is not excuse enough to allow public men to trample upon the sensibilities and sensitivities of those who are neither public men nor so blissfully dumb. What ignorance needs for the next inevitable occasion for insult is some advice for it, which, if followed, would spare us all further injury.

Perhaps some hon. members might take the sound wisdom of a jock — a good man like Sam Rutigliano, the coach of the Cleveland Browns. Sam's wisdom is handed down from his father, a truck driver. As he told a reporter last week, "My dad gave me the best advice I've ever had: 'If ever you have an opportunity to keep your mouth shut, take advantage of it.' "

Too bad Sam's dad never ran for Parliament.

26 December 1980

"Welcome to the eighties," the man said — his first words to the country on the night of his return from limbo, some ten months ago. P.E. Trudeau greeted the new decade with all the relish of a miraculous survivor who had enjoyed the luck of falling from his office window and landing on Joe Clark. Considering his good fortune, Trudeau's implied endorsement of the new decade is understandable: where he had once feared he would spend it in ignominy, he can now look ahead to more years of celebrity.

You do not have to be right to survive in politics — historic examples abound as testimony to that — but you do need luck. No one could deny that the prime minister has had enough luck in 1980 to be overdrawn on his account. Forty-five percent of Canadians, say the polls, think he is doing a good job, a judgment that can only be considered fortuitous, given the record. Not only is that percentage remarkably high for any elected politician these days, it looks even higher when compared to the scores of Ed Broadbent, who is a distant second, and Joe Clark, who is dead last.

For Conservatives, ever relentless scorekeepers, the prime minister's acceptance rating defies explanation. They have, as well, other numbers written on their cuffs — rates of inflation, unemployment and interest — and they add to these the awesome folly of the last federal budget and the growing opposition to the constitutional proposals. After that, they are driven to hard questions and strong drink.

The hardest of all questions as to the anomalous condition of the Tory party concerns the leadership of Clark. Could there be, Conservatives ask themselves, some correlation between the unlikely popularity of the prime minister, despite considerable and compelling reasons for it to be otherwise, and the negative public perception of the alternative to Trudeau — namely Clark? Is the Tory leader all that is keeping Trudeau up?

Were this as true as the evidence suggests, Clark cannot survive the confidence vote at the Tory general meeting in late February, and the party will be heading for a leadership convention as inevitably as it will be heading for the month of March.

I suppose I spend as much time listening to Tories, or hearing from them, as anyone who is not legally domiciled with them. One such, a member of caucus during the inter-regnum of 1979-80, who then lost his seat, has come to the sorrowful conclusion that the party has no other choice than to start over again with a new leader.

"Here we are," he said, "with everything going for us and we're going nowhere. Supposing Clark was a football coach whose team hadn't won a game for a year. What would you do?"

When I suggested that, further to his sporting analogy, maybe the team needed a better offensive line, his answer was that the Tory party had never been so deep in experience and talent as it is today. ("We've got privy councillors coming out of our ears.") And when I reminded him that public opinion seemed to be coming Clark's way on the constitutional issue, he parried with a question: "Why doesn't some of that come to Clark himself?"

When I asked a provincial party organizer how Clark was doing in the opinion of the rank-and-file, the discreet answer was a slow shake of the head with eyes looking to the ceiling. Plainly, the situation for the Tory leader is somewhere between desperate and hopeless.

The canvass against Clark has been a quiet one, as the vote against him will be. Apart from the party's lunatic fringe, no one feels the need to mobilize opposition to his leadership. The present mood of the party is easy to misread since so many are simply resigned to what they feel is an inevitability, however much they regret it, or would wish it otherwise.

These are the harsh realities of contemporary politics, and much of the reason why so many prefer to keep their distance from it. But if we knew why so much of the country had made up its mind about Clark — which is why a number of his party also have — we would then understand both the country and the Tory party, each similarly divided, better than we do. Of that, and of Clark himself, more later.

17 February 1981

John Nance Garner, otherwise known as "Cactus Jack" and a former vice-president of the United States, was once asked to evaluate the high office he held.

"It ain't worth a cup of warm spit," Garner answered, speaking of an exalted position no more than a heartbeat away, as they say, from the presidency of the Great Republic. Others within earshot of this exchange later testified that "Cactus Jack" didn't exactly say that, but the reported version was as near to being accurate as could be reproduced in family newspapers.

Garner has long since departed for the Valhalla reserved for honest appraisers, but his truth goes marching on. In this age of enlightenment, his wisdom ought to enjoy even wider application.

There are at present three candidates running for the office of president of the National Association of the Conservative Party: Peter Blaikie, a Montreal lawyer and unsuccessful federal Tory candidate; Pat Nowlan, a Nova Scotia MP since 1965; and Chris Speyer, MP for Cambridge, Ontario since 1979. All three are running hard, as if their lives depended on winning, and as though they'd never heard of John Nance Garner.

The office of national president bears no prize, other than the title, an executive assistant and travelling-around money. The hired hand and the expense account are relatively new perquisites of office and represent a considerable departure from the days of J.M. Macdonnell, who held the post in the 1950s, and who not only considered it his duty to raise money for the party but to pay his own way in the process. As with much else these days, bargains like that are hard to find.

It used to be that a man did not run for the position of national president but that the position pursued the man. It usually took a good deal of arm-twisting to get anyone to take it. But that process ended after Macdonnell laid down his burden and Gordon Churchill agreed to take it up, only to find George Hees running against him. After Hees had won, the office assumed far greater importance in the party and provided Tories with more frequent opportunity to indulge in their favourite activity, which is to draw their own blood. More often than not, the contest for the party presidency tends to be a leadership convention in miniature.

Occasionally, the fight for the presidency has been a proxy war between elements within the party and over issues larger than the candidates themselves. Hees won, as did Egan Chambers later on, because the delegates suspected their opponents in both contests had been hand-picked by the party "establishment." Rebellion comes as naturally to Tories as singing does to birds and no candidate for the Tory presidency in modern practice could survive the public endorsement of his party's leader.

This brings us to Messrs. Speyer, Nowlan and Blaikie, each of whom would like to win without much visible help from Joe Clark. Both Speyer and Blaikie have confessed they are voting against a leadership convention, although Speyer says that, if elected, he would convene another general meeting of the party "within a reasonable period of time, possibly eighteen months." In short, if you elect Speyer, you'll get another shot at Clark before the next election.

Nowlan is mute on the subject of leadership review — well, almost. In order to help bind up the wounds after the leadership decision is made, he's staying neutral so as not to, in the candidate's words, "cheese off" anyone by taking a public position. And Blaikie, while backing Clark, says he objects to candidates being linked with pro- or anti-Clark factions.

Since the reasons why any of these gentlemen are seeking the office has thus far remained obscure, rumour fills the void of mystery. Speyer is alleged to be a stalking-horse for the leadership ambitions of David Crombie, his caucus colleague. Blaikie is rumoured to be a front-man for Clark. Nowlan is suspected by some of being a clone of Robert Coates, the retiring national president.

Apart from these allegations, each man has professed value to the party. Nowlan has lived on both coasts in Nova Scotia and British Columbia, and thus knows the country. Speyer comes from Ontario, where the Tories have to win to hope to govern. Blaikie comes from Quebec, a province with fewer members in the Tory caucus than there are from the Yukon. What they have in common is that each wants to be national president.

You can imagine what "Cactus Jack" Garner would say about that.

Not always on the right side, John Diefenbaker would often say about himself, but never on the side of wrong. The adage must be one handed down from the elders in the politics of Saskatchewan, for the same could have been said of Tommy Douglas, a former premier of the province, and also said of Allan Blakeney, the much admired, widely praised, and highly esteemed premier of Saskatchewan. Out there in the great Canadian wheat belt, they also grow virtuous men for the mills of Canadian politics.

All three could only be considered virtuous public men in the literal sense. They were also Baptists, and each was born elsewhere — Diefenbaker in Ontario, Douglas in Scotland, and Blakeney in Nova Scotia. The analogies do not end there: the three men have been articulate, resonant, if not voluble, orators and each of them, for a significant period of time, have been the beneficiaries of media adoration. Diefenbaker and Douglas both began their careers in provincial politics and went on to lead national parties in the House of Commons: that Blakeney will follow the same route is widely believed not only to be a foregone conclusion, but inevitable. Among all the premiers, he has, by far, the largest interest in a national political party.

As a politician, however, the differences between Blakeney and his notable predecessors outnumber the resemblances. While cut from the same cloth, the premier of Saskatchewan is very much a modern politician, supple, resilient, adroit, intelligent, and, among his peers, a man of inexhaustible good will. As for Diefenbaker's stricture — never being on the side of wrong — Blakeney has refined it further: he is seldom clearly seen on any side. In the abyss created by the polarity between federal and provincial positions on the constitution, he has managed to straddle both sides, a trick that has earned him both envy and admiration and, politics being what it is, some whispered resentment.

Blakeney alone, among the provincial premiers, has carved out a role which has made him persona grata to all sides. Inescapably a member of the western alliance, he is considered by Ontario the most responsible and flexible of the four western premiers. And although six of the ten provincial governments have joined to challenge the federal constitutional proposals in the courts, Saskatchewan is included among "The Gang of Four" (the others being Ontario, New Brunswick and Nova Scotia) who are either supporting the proposals or expressing their objections by other means.

"A socialist Bill Davis," said an Ontario senior civil servant, bestowing the ultimate compliment. If you put Davis in the premier's office in Regina, he went on to say, and installed Blakeney at Queen's

Park, and no one was allowed to look behind the doors, both governments would continue to run much the same as they are now.

But though Davis supports the federal government's constitutional proposals, with reservations, and Blakeney supports some and opposes others, also with reservations, it is Davis who has taken the heat from his own supporters, some of the media, and even from a fellow Tory premier, New Brunswick's Richard Hatfield. Davis's position has been called "statesmanlike" by the Ottawa *Citizen* and the *Peterborough Examiner*, among others, but he has the lumps to show for it. Blakeney, also wearing the mantle of statesman, hasn't a mark on him.

To Ontario, Blakeney appears as the only premier with whom it can speak in candour, and Davis does so frequently. Whether as socialist or federalist, Blakeney nonetheless seems to have accepted Ontario's minimal postion with respect to energy policy, which is that some of the profits now going to the producing provinces and the multinationals ought to be diverted into a central fund — however administered — for development and exploration.

As for Blakeney's constitutional posture, Ontario is convinced he would like to be more supportive of the federal government, but feels he can be more effective, and helpful, by "free-wheeling."

"What he does," explained a Queen's Park observer, "is continually conditionalize his support. He does this by appearing to move closer to Ottawa's position, as the feds make concessions, while never appearing entirely satisfied. Blakeney will be the last one to say. 'Okay, that's it.' There will always be one more condition."

While his lines are open to the east, Blakeney is careful to keep in touch with his western compatriots, sometimes not without effort. Premier Bill Bennett invited Alberta's Peter Lougheed to British Columbia to meet privately with his cabinet; after Lougheed had complied, Blakeney was quickly on the phone to Edmonton. Lougheed dutifully made a similar pilgrimage to Regina. "No one makes any end runs around Allan," commented a fellow premier.

But yes, Blakeney is a man sensitive to his unique place on the present scene. A socialist premier in a passel of conservatives, he travels outside his province as a resolute pragmatist. "His instincts," Richard Hatfield says of him, "are very good, his purposes are noble, but he is as much a pragmatist as the rest of us."

Another puts it somewhat differently: "Allan is a modern, contemporary politician with a wide streak of Tammany Hall."

Asked what that means, the answer is that while Blakeney has carefully tended his image as a man of sensible ideas and high ideals, in earnest search of conciliation and compromise, eager to join in consensus, the real politician in him reveals him as merely elusive.

One key to understanding Allan Blakeney is to bear in mind his national ambitions. Few provincial politicians are less reluctant to involve themselves in national issues and national politics. (Not all of them, of course, are given much chance.)

Gerald Regan, as premier of Nova Scotia, would bring his personal hairdresser to Ottawa for a First Ministers' Conference; Blakeney brings his own interviewer, who packages instant (and exclusive) interviews with him for distribution back home. So that when the premier of Saskatchewan emerges from a business dinner at Sussex Drive, the first thing he does is talk to a tape-recorder. Blakeney provides the answers; the questions can be asked later.

And he is no less diligent when in Regina. On the night of the vote on the Quebec Referendum, the premier of Saskatchewan was the only first minister who spent the evening in the company of his advisors, in his office, hearing the returns, and preparing a statement.

"He not only wants to be the first, but he wants to be the most," an associate has said of him. "He wants to be the premier of Saskatchewan AND. . ."

At First Ministers' Conferences, where Blakeney shines, his performance reminds one of theatre-in-the-round. He never forgets his audiences: the one in Saskatchewan, the national audience behind the cameras, and the other one in the stalls, the New Democrats. He does not turn his back to any of them for long. In almost every Blakeney peroration or formal statement, there are morsels of reassurance for everyone: yes, he is a westerner; yes, he is a Canadian federalist; and yes, there is something to be said for Newfoundland's position, for Alberta's, Nova Scotia's, Quebec's, Trudeau's — and his own, which is never quite the same as anyone else's.

"The one thing you have to learn about Blakeney," says a civil servant from another province who has been around at many a meeting, "is that you can never be sure just where he's at. Just when you think you understand his position, you find out you don't."

He is a man of nuance. On the issue of the entrenchment of language rights, Blakeney has come some distance, or a little, or none — it depends on what you read between the lines. At the premiers' conference held in St. Andrews four years ago, an effort was made to reach consensus on the matter of French and English language rights in education. There was an assumption that Lévesque would not go along, and he didn't, and a worry that Davis wouldn't either (he did), but an assumption also that Blakeney would.

When a prepared, and precirculated, statement on the subject came before the premiers, Blakeney, to the surprise of some, expressed misgivings. His reservations reflected a concern for the multicultural communities in Saskatchewan. In the end, a conference observer recalls, "the best effort" draft was abandoned for a watered-down version.

Blakeney rarely embarks on the subject of language rights without first tipping his hat to the "multicultural diversity" of Saskatchewan. This may be, as someone suggested, because, as a Maritimer, he is still uncomfortable with that aspect of Saskatchewan politics or, as likely, he is knowing enough of western opinion on "language rights" — meaning French — that he will take some pains to assure his constituents that he hasn't forgotten, when in Ottawa, who they are.

In Ottawa, during the penultimate First Ministers' Conference on the constitution, Blakeney addressed himself to the issue (after first citing his province's "strong multicultural tradition"):

"I do say, however, what I have said on earlier occasions, that this question of language rights is not a question only of responding to the groups within our province, but also is, as I have phrased it on other occasions, part of the confederation bargain. I do not regard this in the same category as other rights, and I have made this point before and I think others know it, and accordingly, while I don't want to go through the paper section by section now, I would simply say that we will be listening to the debate and generally will be responsive to the idea of incorporating some language guarantees."

There are only two sentences in that statement but three separate instances in which Blakeney inserts reminders that what he is saying he has said before. But then, what is he saying?

"I would simply say that we will be listening to the debate and *generally* will be responsive to the *idea* of incorporating *some* language guarantees."

The prime minister, perhaps as much at sea after that as anyone, pressed him further:

"Including the area of education, or would you rather leave that?"

To which Blakeney replied, "I would rather leave that, but I certainly don't exclude it."

Still, a viewer watching these proceedings from his armchair could only sense the deftness, poise and the radiant spirit of the man and conclude that Blakeney and the prime minister of Canada were almost, if not quite, on all fours on language rights.

Perhaps they are. On 9 October 1980, in a statement issued in response to the tabling of the federal resolution on the constitution in Parliament, Blakeney could say, "Saskatchewan supports the entrenching in the constitution of *reasonable* provisions respecting language rights in primary and secondary schools. We regard the proposals on these language rights as *generally* acceptable." (Emphasis mine.)

Eighteen days later, speaking in Halifax, Blakeney wasted fewer words; in fact, wasted none: "I therefore favour the inclusion of language rights in the constitution." Such lack of equivocation would indicate he had come some distance since St. Andrews or, perhaps, it was merely that he was speaking some distance from Regina.

But of course, between 9 and 29 October 1980, there was 21 October, the date on which Trudeau and NDP leader Ed Broadbent "cut a deal," as they say, on a matter of vital concern to Saskatchewan — described in Blakeney's subsequent words as "the inclusion of a resources section in the federal resolution on the constitution." While the deal was made by Trudeau with Broadbent, no one doubts that the premier of Saskatchewan was party to it. More likely, Broadbent was holding Blakeney's proxy.

The federal resolution, on 9 October, was "inconsistent with our historical traditions, and with our present conception of Canada as a federal state," according to Blakeney, who added, "I want to leave no doubt of my strong objection to the unilateral nature of [the] proposed action."

Besides, the resolution "contains nothing urged by the governments of the western provinces." Even so, a man who prefers to have an oar in all boats was not going overboard on the issue: his government would, he said, take "the interim position of reserving its decision to oppose or support the resolution," at least until there could be consultation with the other premiers. Shortly after that, and after six of Blakeney's colleagues agreed to take the matter to court, Trudeau made an offer Broadbent could not refuse.

Nor could Blakeney, altogether. The new provisions, pertaining to provincial powers over resources, "will go some way towards achieving the objectives we have sought in constitutional negotiations," he said, in a statement issued the next day.

But then: "They do not, however, go all the way. . .We have reserved our decision on whether to support or oppose the federal resolution. We are encouraged by this important indication of flexibility. But we continue to reserve our decision."

If "conditionalize" is not yet an accepted verb, it will become one before Allan Blakeney is done with politics. He has raised conditionalizing to an art form, and become the master of the hard bargain. As to the latter, there is ample evidence of his ability to make the most of his opportunities simply by always appearing as a man with his options open. Put another way, as a premier at the federal-provincial table, he is not so much flexible as he is fluid.

In 1975, the premiers assembled at their annual gathering in St. John's on that occasion to exhort the federal government to take strong measures to stem inflation — including that of implementing wage and price controls. During the in-camera proceedings, all premiers present, including Blakeney, were agreed on the need for controls. But when a draft recommendation to the prime minister was before them, Blakeney was among those to argue against so specific a proposal. In the end, the premiers sent off a letter to Trudeau saying only, in effect, "do something."

But a federal observer had also been present at the St. John's gathering (and for the last time). Weeks later, on Thanksgiving day, having invited the premiers to Sussex Drive, Trudeau raised the matter of wage and price controls, informing them he knew they had all supported it at their meeting in Newfoundland. He asked for their renewed support for the policy. Tacitly, or otherwise, all agreed.

Before the meeting ended, however, Blakeney requested a private audience with the prime minister and the two men withdrew. Returning to the room, a witness recalls, "It was obvious they had made a deal, something to do with transportation rates. Anyway, all I remember was talk about twenty-five cents, or five cents — whatever. But they had made a deal."

There is this uncanny ability to wring concessions from consensus. Nothing entirely novel in that, one could say, but the story is not yet finished: within weeks of Trudeau's announcement of controls, Blakeney had become a vocal critic of the policy.

The premier of Saskatchewan is not an easy read: behind the avuncular mask of the conciliator lurks the alert opportunist. Still, it has been said of him that, beyond the borders of his province, he has no enemies. "Even Noranda likes him," was the grudging admission of one of his fellow premiers.

Allan Blakeney is liked even by those who are unnerved by him. His fondness for detail, his habit of telling you more than you need to know — "Ask him the time of day and he'll give you the history of Switzerland" — taken with his quick-silver elusiveness, are the qualities of a man to be respected, even admired, even if rarely sought out for the pleasure of his company. (Jean-Luc Pepin once idly asked a question as to how many railroads had been privately owned at the time of Confederation. Someone responded that he could only recall the Inter-Colonial Railway as one. Remembers another who was present, "Blakeney overheard the question and proceeded to list all the railways in Canada and where they ran. He left Pepin in a daze.")

During this uneasy time of "constitutional interruptus" — an Ontario descriptive term — Blakeney's political stock continues to rise. So long as a good part of the country sees unanimity as the ultimate safeguard in any constitutional rearrangement, there will be a hammerlock on change. Blakeney remains, during this period, the lynch-pin and catalyst-apparent, moving nimbly among the various factions and forces and the several regions, criss-crossing party lines, serving as conduit, lightning rod, friend in court and arbiter of the worth of trial balloons. No one quite understands his value, yet none dispute it.

"I just want to add that I share a number of the views expressed," Allan Blakeney said — ever agreeable — to his fellow first ministers, addressing himself to the agenda item concerning the preamble to the constitution.

"I would like to think," he went on, "that we could have a preamble which would be an uplifting and educational document. We take the view that we can probably accept almost any preamble that meets with the view of the other first ministers and will therefore reserve."

To which Trudeau, as chairman, responded. "Well, that is pretty cunning. In view of the fact the premier knows very well there will be disagreement between at least two first ministers here and maybe at some point we will either decide not to have a preamble or you will have to take sides."

Before the Parliamentary Committee on the Constitution, on the last day before the Christmas adjournment, Blakeney came to Ottawa as both Grinch and Santa Claus: tough, conciliatory, optimistic, concerned, wildly impractical ("Let's return to the bargaining table"), but shrewd: forty-six pages of bafflegab for those who are still trying to find Saskatchewan's bottom line.

A Dalhousie Law School classmate described Blakeney, the student, as "one of the boys who was not one of the boys." Asked about Blakeney's oft-proclaimed intellectual powers, he replied, "The guy's not just an intellectual, he's also very bright."

His unique influence among the premiers, and in Ottawa, is not the singular accomplishment of a politician with the smarts, but represents as well the acknowledgment by his peers of Saskatchewan's "deferred" power — an awareness of the emergence in the 1980s of another economic giant in the West, one rich in wheat, oil and potash, richer still for the benefit of having been a spectator to the explosive growth in neighbouring Alberta. Among the many things people tell you about the premier of Saskatchewan, the most perceptive may be the one that says, "Allan Blakeney is a Peter Lougheed with Lougheed's experience."

Meanwhile, just as this goes to press, the prime minister is at Sussex Drive, awaiting word from the premier of Saskatchewan, who is in Hawaii. Trudeau and his officials believe final agreement is at hand following a round of intensive negotiations over the constitutional package. And yes — comes the word at last from the beach at Waikiki — Blakeney is willing.

But there is just one more matter, before all is agreed upon, and it has to do with the Senate. Would the prime minister agree to. . . .

The prime minister's instant reaction is unknown, and anyway perhaps unprintable. The rest is history.*

28 May 1981

My first encounter with David Lewis was just that — a brief verbal shoving match, something of a joust, while he was sitting in a barber's chair being made up for a television appearance, and I was awaiting my turn.

He did not, he told me, think highly of advertising since it extolled the virtues of everything, whether or not there were any. As for the growing presence of advertising in politics, he was particularly concerned about that. Advertising men, he suspected, were long on techniques but short on principles.

Since at the time — this was early on in the sixties — I was as much into advertising as into politics, I felt as though David Lewis had just put an elbow in my ribs. I recall then saying to him that I thought as highly of lawyers as he did of advertising men, and had in mind lawyers such as those who were retained by trade union racketeers to keep them out of jail.

Understandably, for some time after on numerous occasions when we met — invariably in television studios — our relationship was, in a word, strained. But there are worse places to get to know some measurement of a man than in tv studios. Lewis was very good before the cameras, largely because he was well-informed, and because he was that rare public man whose mind always ran well ahead of his tongue. After a while, I developed a healthy and unreserved respect for him, until finally I could say I liked him.

I suppose my own perceptions of Lewis changed no more than he himself did. It did seem early on in his career as a national figure in politics that he had no doubts about anything, more particularly his socialist views. Such assurance created an aura of piety about him and the strong impression of a man who believed himself possessed of certain inalienable truths; he sometimes sounded as though he might be in danger of becoming virtuous to a fault.

But the earlier David Lewis mellowed, as his experience in the realities of Canadian politics broadened, as he became — like anyone else would become in the system — so often confronted by the agony of choices, not simply between right and wrong, but between shades of gray, even between bad or worse. It was as though the more he learned

*These final paragraphs were not, as I believed, written just as the piece went to press, but — alas — after it had already gone.

57

of the coarse grain of real politics, and was obliged to cope with it, the more humble, human and compassionate he became.

He was perhaps the most powerful of all the national leaders of his party: others have had influence, Lewis had leverage. After the 1972 Liberal débâcle, which left P.E. Trudeau clinging to a precarious minority in Parliament, Lewis shored up the government, even though he genuinely admired Robert Stanfield and genuinely did not admire Trudeau.

But as he explained afterwards — indeed, on the occasion of our last meeting earlier this year in Toronto — he kept Trudeau in power and held him in ransom, wringing from the government measures for which we are still paying. It was that brief interlude in Canadian politics in which organ-grinder and monkey jokes became common-place — and David Lewis called the tune to which the Liberal monkey danced.

Thus, in the critical years of his leadership of a national party, Lewis found himself not as an earnest ideologue but as a power-broker. He discovered himself supporting a politician he mistrusted and disliked — Trudeau — and denying opportunity to a man he admired and respected — Stanfield. Years later, he would say, truthfully, that the choice had to do with the interests of his party, for which he had given and spent the lion's share of his life and vitality.

He put it very simply. Had he allowed the circumstances for a Stanfield minority government in 1972, the Tories would have soon called a general election and, in his words, "our party would have been wiped out." It was a lesson he had learned in 1963, when the Diefenbaker minority government fell, and even David Lewis lost his seat in Toronto.

What was endearing, touching and admirable about Lewis was his ultimate humanity. For all his intellectual gifts, debating skills, and partisan zealousness, he became much like the rest of us — plagued with doubts, unsure, and steering by stars of a private, troubled conscience, sometimes obscured in the darkness of power politics. To the end, he was a party man; understandable, in that building and shaping it had been his life's work. David Lewis was also a world-class politician, and it was among the gifts of the times to have known him.

1 August 1981

This is not meant as requiem for E. Davie Fulton; but as his name surfaced once more in the media, following his resignation from the bench in British Columbia, I was reminded of his remarkable career and the example it offers of how politics can consume able men, just as mediocre ones are so often preserved.

No Canadian politician could have possessed better qualifications for public life than Davie Fulton. Both his grandfather and great-uncle had been premiers of British Columbia. His father had been a provincial minister of the Crown. A Rhodes scholar and lawyer, and with five years of war service, Fulton was first elected to the House of Commons in 1945, at twenty-nine years of age clearly a man of considerable promise. He soon became president of the Young Progressive Conservatives and the darling of the Tory party. In 1956, he contested the leadership of the party at the convention which chose John Diefenbaker. A year later, he was minister of justice in the first Diefenbaker government.

Fulton attracted a number of bright young men to his employ, among them Michael Pitfield, Marc Lalonde and Lowell Murray. In his memoirs, Diefenbaker noted Fulton's predilection for hiring "Liberals" and, as well, wrote that he had detected in Fulton the personal defect of "ambition." In the Tory minority government of 1962, Fulton was given Public Works, an appointment everyone, including himself, saw as a demotion, and one many Tories came to resent because of the minister's stubborn indifference to considerations of patronage.

No longer the darling of his party and conspicuously out of favour with his prime minister, it seemed Davie Fulton had fallen victim to Murphy's Law — anything that could go wrong, did. In 1963, his British Columbian friends persuaded him to abandon federal politics to take over the leadership of the provincial party — then, as now, in bankruptcy. He involved himself in the abortive cabinet revolt against Diefenbaker and, in the federal election that followed, sat out the campaign — at least, according to Diefenbaker.

I recall being at Sussex Drive with the prime minister and Howard Green at the outset of the campaign.

"Where's Fulton?" Diefenbaker asked of Green.

"I don't know," Green answered truthfully.

"I'll tell you where he is," the prime minister roared. "He's sitting on his ass in Salmon Arm!"

Wherever he was, Fulton was surely in the wilderness. His foray into provincial politics proved an unmitigated disaster. In 1965, as the party's national president and at the urging of his supporters, I made a public appeal to Fulton to return to federal politics. Diefenbaker, interpreting the invitation as an act of disloyalty, was outraged. Anyway, Fulton returned and was elected again in his old seat of Kamloops.

Once more, in 1967, Fulton contested the party leadership, running a strong third, and supported by Murray, Joe Clark, Brian Mulroney, and Alan Eagleson, among others. After that, and twenty-two years after his emergence as a public figure, he came to be considered a spent force in politics.

If football is a game of inches, politics is a game of luck, and both offer a paradise for second-guessers. Fulton has been second-guessed by just about everyone, from Diefenbaker to the late Mr. Justice Spence, in his report on the so-called "security" aspect of the Munsinger affair. For all his obvious abilities, intellect and drive, the ultimate verdict on Fulton as a politician is that he lacked judgment.

Far more likely, it seems to me, is that Fulton's brilliant promise was consumed in the raging passions of the so-called Diefenbaker years, which are now ritually trivialized by a mysteriously obsequious media and which still await the more honest appraisal of history.

The greater truth is that those years scarred the lives and destroyed the public careers of many worthy, able men and women — too many and too painful to enumerate. None was more able nor more worthy than Fulton, who only shared with them the misfortune of wasting a good part of his life in a period of Canadian politics darkened by malignity and madness.

Looking back on it now, it strikes me that what we all owe to Fulton is not any requiem but, instead, an apology.

Divided We Stand

26 November 1976

The national television networks presented a colloquium the other night featuring all the tribal chieftains — Prime Minister P.E. Trudeau, Opposition Leader Joe Clark, NDP Leader Ed Broadbent, and — um — a Mr. Fortin, whose role and place still seem to me obscure. Each of them addressed themselves to the subject of Quebec, and what to do, now that voters there have elected a party to office whose principal purpose is to take the province out of Confederation.

The prime minister, in the parlance used to describe football quarterbacks, is a scrambler. He is elusive, all over the field, a moving target, and a man not easy to bring down.

The recent result in Quebec, he told us, dropping back, shows how strong democracy is these days. Think of it: a party that was nowhere in 1970 is now the government of Quebec, and it's only 1976.

Indeed, it is impressive. In 1970, Quebeckers gave the Parti Quebecois some 662,500 of their votes; in 1976, it gave them some 1,370,000 votes. The prime minister explained this meteoric rise as due to the fact that, in 1970 and 1973, the Parti Quebecois campaigned on the issue of separatism. (Even so, in 1973, their vote rose to 898,000.) Rounding out his syllogism, he concluded that the reason the Parti Quebecois won this time was because they did not campaign on the issue of separatism.

I have trouble with the prime minister's quod erat demonstrandum, but then so have I often. In this instance, I have trouble with a corollary which he omitted, which is that the Liberal Party was roundly endorsed in 1970 and 1973, when it campaigned against separatism, as it did again in 1976, when it was roundly trounced. So far as the Liberal Party was concerned, the issue of separatism has been predominant in each of the last three campaigns. How was it, then, that Quebeckers voted so emphatically for the Liberals, and against separatism, in two elections, and then voted just as emphatically against the Liberals in the third election?

Well, the prime minister is now on the other side of the field, still looking for an open receiver. Morality! That's it, democracy and morality. To explain the shift in votes, from 1970 to 1976, from the Liberals to the Parti Quebecois, the prime minister testified that it was not creeping separatism in Quebec, but creeping morality. This reasoned result, he said, is not only a splendid example of democracy in Quebec but a vigorous expression of Quebec's belief in political morality.

A lot of us could go along with that, but even allowing it as a credible supposition, how was it that the prime minister — in the course of the provincial election campaign — said he hoped and thought Bourassa would win? And how was it that his loyal lieutenant and friend Jean Marchand would take himself to Quebec and enter the fray as a Liberal candidate?

Plainly, there has been a recent time when the prime minister and many of his federal colleagues were squarely on the side of immorality or, put otherwise, when they were hoping that morality would not be so all-important that the PQ would win. Some may find this confusing. Others will find it cynical.

Still on his feet, the prime minister moved to appeal for a confederation in which Quebeckers would be "as at home in Vancouver or Toronto as in Quebec City."

If we are to survive this crisis, the very best thing we could do, at the outset, is to avoid setting objectives that are not only impossible of achievement, but as well defy the Canadian character.

We are, as Canadians, the children of our regions, culture and history. So that when I say I am at home in Jemseg, N.B., and less at home in Quebec City, Hamilton, Moose Jaw and Vancouver, and positively uneasy in Prince Albert, it is not the result of a flawed citizenship, or the cultural deprivations of other places, but the confirmation of a personal history. It's the way it is.

What the prime minister is saying is that he has a dream of having all of us live one day under the same roof of some monstrous national Holiday Inn, called Canada. None of us, and especially Mr. Trudeau, should be attempting the impossible. The difficult will be hard enough.

"The crisis is now," the prime minister said, which was the only inarguable statement of the evening. He then added that Canada "must not. . . survive by force."

What one finds disturbing in the statement is that the prime minister found it necessary to say it. Perhaps it's all to the good that while discussing the unthinkable one might as well mention the unmentionable, which is the application of force to prevent it. Just the same, it seems awfully early in the game to raise that sort of conjecture, and one is puzzled by what appears to be the present state of mind, up there in Ottawa, which suggests they are already considering contingencies for when the referendum is lost.

If the prime minister is a scrambler, then the opposition leader is a man who stays in the pocket. There seem to be many who believe the issue of separatism has mostly to do with regional disparity, which is to suggest that national unity comes only when there is a chicken in every pot. In the instance of Quebec, I seriously doubt it.

Still, Clark had the best and most warming line of the night, which was something about a Canada that succeeded "not just as a country, but as a place to live." Clark did not say much, representing himself as a man for all regions, but he said that, and I, for one, believe he has something there.

18 December 1976

On 13 December (mark the date) 1976, the prime minister of Canada, P.E. Trudeau, and the nine premiers of the provinces who wish to remain in confederation, met at dinner with the tenth premier, who doesn't. The official host was P.E. Trudeau; after all, it's his dining room, and a pleasant one with a nice view not overlooking the pool.

The tenth premier, for those reading this in Sri Lanka, is René Lévesque, a new boy in the club and anxious not to become an old boy at such affairs. But at least the premier of Quebec agreed to come, which might have accounted for the saumon fumé Gaspésie on the menu.

The evening provided both a square meal and an agenda — a nocturnal version of the business lunch. Even so, politicians dining in the company of a celebrity are likely to become restless with an agenda. René Lévesque is a celebrity and recognized as such by his dinner companions.

The formality of his shaking hands with the prime minister of Canada — confederation's first golden handshake, perhaps — was a media event. Furthermore, the mere presence of Lévesque at the conference had brought celebrity to the rest of them — have we ever heard and seen so much of Allan Blakeney?

It's the sort of celebrity that might come to the boarders at the YMCA the morning after Faye Dunaway had spent the night there. But now gathered about the Trudeau dining table, making small talk and minor progress, restlessness gathered after the fish and during the veal. It was then that Frank Moores, the premier of Newfoundland, took the plunge.

Moores is a man who does not enjoy being bored and, whether he is dining with René Lévesque or Faye Dunaway, he is not going to be encumbered by someone else's tedious agenda. So, Moores put it to René Lévesque, declaring himself as one proud and happy to be a Canadian (Newfoundlanders, of course, have had the shortest experience), and did Mr. Lévesque realize what he was doing to the country, by which, Moores explained, he meant did Lévesque realize what he was doing to the bond market in the United States?

This, as they say, set the cat among the pigeons. But Lévesque was, in his way, reassuring. He replied that he shared Moores's concern and that he, Lévesque, planned to visit the financial capitals to ease apprehensions about the consequences of separation to Quebec and Canada. To which Richard Hatfield, the premier of New Brunswick, replied that he planned to visit the province of Quebec and do much the same, but with opposite intentions. That, said Lévesque, would be all right by him.

By now, almost everyone joined the conversation, with two exceptions. One of these was the prime minister, who had assumed the lotus position, looking inscrutable, saying nothing.

The other exception was Ontario's William Davis, who reminded his colleagues that such matters being discussed were not on the agenda and had, indeed, been strenuously excised from it. The voice of Ontario is invariably businesslike, reasonable, and unheeded.

The premier of Prince Edward Island had not been the most voluble of the premiers, but he had a question. Alex Campbell wanted to know if Lévesque really meant what he had been saying about independence, and all that. The question seemed to startle Lévesque, as it stunned some others. But sometimes naïveté can be rewarding.

"My intentions," he told them, "are to get out."

And there it was, straight from the source, naked of any caveat, without embellishment, unlike the roomier, more familiar political statements which come furnished with escape hatches, trapdoors, two-way mirrors, and attics stuffed with qualifications, reservations and packaged fog.

The premier of Manitoba, Ed Schreyer, wanted to know when the independence referendum would be held. Any time, answered Lévesque.

This month?

This month, he was told, or next month, or sometime after that. He couldn't say. After all, someone said to Ed Schreyer, are you going to tell us when you're going to call your election? But the reality is, the referendum date could be important, whether you're Frank Moores going to the bond market, or Ed Schreyer going to the people. Or P.E. Trudeau, who maintains his silence, appearing to be into transcendental meditation.

Someone suggested an hypothesis: What if the independence referendum were lost? What would Lévesque do? Memories vary in recalling the answer. One witness remembers only that the answer was confusing, in that Lévesque seemed to be speaking to two possibilities, either losing the referendum or losing an election, but he referred to his age, the years given to the struggle, and the sense of it was that a time would come when younger, fresher forces must take up the torch.

Having been asked about patriation of the constitution, Lévesque opined that he did not give it much importance. Well, since it wasn't important to him, would he then not stand in the way of it? Lévesque was not about to go that far, it was only that the government of Quebec had many more pressing questions than that of the constitution of a country they were anxious to get out of.

The prime minister, seeming to have heard all he wanted to hear — or concluding everyone else had — adjourned his meeting to the parlour where, with his spectacles perched low on his nose, like Saint Nicholas himself, he read a three-page document, which would become tomorrow's grand compromise on the end of revenue guarantees and would proclaim the bright new doctrine of flexibility. But by this time, Lévesque had departed, pleading another engagement.

3 May 1977

The prime minister, P.E. Trudeau, has a gift for lapidary expressions, as witness the recent remark that "if English Canada were not so damned obtuse. . . they would have understood this, twenty, thirty, forty years ago." (The subject here, of course, is the Great Canadian Crisis.)

What it was that English Canada has not yet understood, after all these years, is not altogether clear. Reading extracts from the transcript of his news conference, held prior to his departure overseas, one concludes that the "this" that anglophones failed to understand can only be his statement, two paragraphs earlier, that "for a hundred — at least fifty — years Quebeckers have been discussing what their place in Canada should be." Admittedly, that is not much to go on, but it is, notwithstanding, the only "this" that could apply to the that, which is English-Canadian obtuseness.

The prime minister does not say things he does not mean to say, a conclusion I have reached after failing to recall anything he ever said that he would later say he wished he had not said, or was sorry to have said. He is also a man who is disdainful of sentiment, emotion, or passion, so that when he seems to be speaking in heat or out of provocation, my hunch is that he already has prepared the outburst, perhaps even rehearsing it before his mirror. As to whether the prime minister really, seriously believes that anglophones have been obtuse for the past forty years is not moot here; you had better believe, however, only that he meant to say it.

I have not been a student of Canadian Liberalism for lo these many years not to have some divinations as to what Liberals are about. Having studied the prime minister's prepared outburst, I am inclined to relate it to high strategy. If all does not come well in the end, in Quebec, and things are not coming well at all at present, the least blameworthy person will be the prime minister, closely followed by the members of the Liberal Party.

All reason and logic would suggest that if indeed Quebec should be lost to Confederation, there could be no greater instrument responsible than the Liberal Party, whose hegemony over that province has been historic and absolute, and, further, no individual could be more to blame than the prime minister, who has been, again historically, unerringly wrong in his assessments of Quebec. But, as we know, the trouble with reason and logic is that they do not matter in politics.

Where the prime minister has been unerringly right has been in his assessments of English-speaking Canada — an abominable but necessary hyphenation — because he has more than once caught its mood and has ridden to power with it, as with his One Canada crusade in 1968, with the "apprehended insurrection" responses in 1970, and again wage and price controls in 1974. What he knows now about Canadian anglophones, confronted with the crisis, is that their essential masochism invests them with a sense of guilt. What have we done to make things go wrong?

Well, we've been damned obtuse, for one thing.

The seeds are being sown now, to take root before, and should ever, winds of recrimination sweep the land. It's our fault, you see, this ultimate impasse that has been gathering for "a hundred — at least fifty — years."

There may even be some truth in it, in the sense that the anglophones, pretty well since the coming to power of Laurier, have abandoned Quebec, its politics, and its place in Canada, to the

Liberal Party. Liberals knew. If they knew nothing else, English-speaking Canada conceded them their wisdom in Quebec.

The concession was not necessarily by choice, but out of political reality. While Liberals told us that only they understood Quebec, they just as emphatically and persistently told the voters of Quebec that we did not understand them. The lynch-pin of Canadian unity came from a Liberal forge. For eighty of the past hundred years, Liberals governed Canada, given the huge majorities from Quebec which made it possible, and chose three French-speaking leaders, each of whom became prime minister.

It may seem obtuse to say it, but there has been a breach of trust here. And what is perhaps as significant a fact as any to be considered is the fact that the Liberal Party has failed in the only enterprise it guaranteed — indeed, in the only thing the country believed it could guarantee — which was to represent the special concerns and interests of Quebec and see them recognized and reconciled within Confederation. Incredibly, the Liberals have lost a game in which they supplied not only all the players, but the umpires too.

Anyone who thinks that's recriminatory has to be obtuse.

6 May 1977

Spring is coming, but slowly, to the Bunker, and its environs. There is too much water in the moat and there is a malfunction in the draw-bridge. But there is no other place I'd rather be after a mind-bending experience in the CBC Ottawa studio, after which the head still reels.

There were three of us in the studio: Blair Neatby, historian, Patrick Watson, author, producer, director, moderator, patron saint of talk shows, and me. Mel Watkins — founding father of the Waffle — was in a Toronto studio, and another historian, Daniel Latouche, who is an ardent separatist, was in Montreal.

The title of the show, I was told, was "Whatever Happened to 1867?" We were invited to be lively and amusing. My abilities to be lively and amusing in such a group seemed inadequate; I was, after all, the only one of them who was not a professor.

At the top of the show, as they say in the trade, we all donned earphones, looking, I would imagine, like a standby crew for "Star Trek." Watson introduced everyone to everyone else, including voices present and voices disembodied, and asked us to listen for a half-hour or so to the voices of P.E. Trudeau, Joe Clark, Ed Broadbent, Marc Lalonde, and a man named Ouellette.

Which we did. They were all talking about the great Canadian crisis. The prime minister was heard speaking to the farmers in Saskatchewan, describing the government of Quebec as the "enemy." Joe Clark followed, saying that was no way to talk about the government of Quebec; such tone and temper would only turn wavering federalists into separatists.

Broadbent then said that Clark and Trudeau were both decentralizers while he, Broadbent, was for a strong central government with matching economic policy. Lalonde came on, sounding like Lalonde — feisty, virtuously right, adamant. (Listening to him I always suspect Lalonde's mind is racing on ahead of his tongue, busily searching for someone else to blame for our present impasse — preferably someone from Ontario, like Bill Davis.) Ouellette said they were all wrong — an observation which, however penetrating, did not make him right either.

By the time they had all spoken several times, the cat had my tongue. What to say about all this? The prime minister's posture is — well — shifty. While the government of Quebec is the "enemy," he goes on to say, as would a good used-car salesman, that no reasonable offer would be refused. He's flexible. The Conservative position is to make a case for further decentralization of the central government. The trouble I have with that is twofold — first, it is strikingly unconservative, in the historic sense; second, I seriously doubt there is much left to decentralize. Joe Clark suggests resources, which would leave the oil to Alberta, the potash to Sakatchewan, the uranium to Quebec and the scenery to the Maritimes.

Ed Broadbent, the NDP leader, seemed the most appealing of them all. Indeed, he seemed more conservative than the Conservatives, more federalist than Lalonde and Trudeau. Obviously, this is nothing if not confusing.

It struck me that all of this is somehow irrelevant to the issue of separatism.

The trouble is that the initiative in the struggle for national survival is all with the government of Quebec. Federalism, since 15 November, has been on the defensive. It is extraordinary that the Canadian government should be debating the merits of an independent Quebec instead of demonstrating the merits of federalism.

Joe Clark may be forgiven his decentralist position; it is the generic function of opposition leaders always to say they would make things better — even federalism — given the chance, and it would be either more or less of it, depending on the climate. The same tolerance is hard to extend to the prime minister and his Quebec lieutenant, for what they are saying, apart from talking tough, is that they will consider any rearrangement of federal powers, provided only that someone else makes them a proposition. This is not so much stonewalling the issue as retreating behind a wall of mush.

Which explains Broadbent's rudimentary appeal. What the country needs is a good, stiff reassertion of federal purpose and action. Perhaps the federal government is saving something for the next election. But the next election is not nearly so important to anyone as is the contest being waged right now in Quebec. We are losing that one, slowly but I fear surely, by default. How can anyone be convinced of the advantages of federalism when most of the talk about federalism is how much less of it we need to survive? Lots and lots of talk, alas, and no action.

14 July 1978

The trouble with nationalism — one of the troubles — is that it cannot be sustained without excess. Nationalism takes root in bigotry, in that compost of hatred, suspicion and ignorance which inevitably produces racism.

Of course, not all bigots are nationalists, nor are all racists, but nationalism is such that it cannot be nurtured and sustained without cultivating, among the population, a racist mentality, which is to say, as the Oxford Dictionary puts it, a "belief in the unchanging fundamental differences between races of men."

The idea is not so barren as to be incapable of ingenious mutation — such as a belief in the fundamental differences between the languages and tongues of men which, in themselves, make men different. Thus, an expression of present-day racism would be the view that the English language is the language of war, weaponry, racism, Little Rock, Watts, Vietnam, Wall Street, exploitative capitalism — in short, the English tongue is the lingua franca of incalculable cruelty and wrongdoing.

Precisely that view was put forward — with strenuous hyperbole — by a woman claiming poetic credentials on the evening of 3 July in Quebec City, at an event billed as "parole et musique," which was part of a provincially sponsored affair called "Fête du Retour aux Sources." The poem, entitled "Speak White," written in free verse, was delivered by the author to a crowd of two thousand, including members of the Quebec government hierarchy, most of whom rewarded the ten-minute reading with a standing ovation interspersed with shouts of "Bravo."

The handful of those in the audience who were English-speaking and who understood what was being said — including the mocking of "the language of Shakespeare, Tennyson and Byron" — were

69

obliged to sit upon their hands, since they had not attended the Fête du Retour aux Sources to be singled out for abuse and insult. A few others, however, did join the applause, out of courtesy and because they had not understood a word of it.

But none of those present enjoyed the performance more than did the front-row group of politicians and other dignitaries, whose enthusiasm for this expression of hatred of the English tongue was nearly uncontained. Among these was the Parti Quebecois Minister of Justice, André Bédard. Thus, for the rest of the two thousand present, it was demonstrably clear that not only was the fête sponsored by the Quebec government, but the opinions expressed were visibly worthy of its patronage. For the elite of the Parti Quebecois, it was satisfying to witness this symbolic merger of the arts and political strategy.

Indeed, the cup runneth over; the tirade that was "Speak White" was followed by a history lesson, delivered by an Indian, who told how his forefathers had joined forces with Montcalm, on the Plains of Abraham, only to have the perfidious British raze their undefended villages and drive women and children into the wilderness. More applause.

Incitements to intolerance, bigotry and hatred are not rare in this country. Nevertheless, it's been some time, if ever, that they were government-sponsored. However, it does seem likely that such excitements must be offered the populace by the present rulers of Quebec if separatism is to succeed.

One makes a mistake to assume that a nationalist government, because it has been democratically elected, is therefore incapable of the habits of tyrants.

Separatism, being a strain of nationalism, has the capacity, as does any other virus of nationalism, to make history and mythology indistinguishable, to propagandize and corrupt generations of the young, and to subvert art and culture to its own purpose.

To begin with, any government which applauds the sentiment that the English language has been the instrument of evil throughout history — and this implies that the French language is in some way superior — such a government is capable of damn near anything.

5 August 1978

A gentleman by the name of Roger Besner has objected to my column of last week in which I gave, as example of the cultivation of racism in Quebec these days, that of a reading of a poem entitled "Speak White" at a public function sponsored by the Parti Quebecois government. Mr. Besner's objection has been lodged with the *Toronto Star*, the Ontario Press Council, the Ontario Human Rights Commission, the Ontario Solicitor-General and the Prime Minister's Office.

It is presumably Mr. Besner's wish that I be purged by the *Star*, drawn by the Human Rights Commission, judged by the solicitor-general, and frowned upon by the prime minister.

One of Mr. Besner's complaints is that I wasn't there when the poem was read, while he was there as "an invited member of the Press Corps." Well, I wasn't there when the *Titanic* went down either, but it will be a long time before anyone sells me a ticket for a crossing.

As to the poem, Mr. Besner would have us believe it's really "a free-verse ode to the little man, the worker, the victim of oppression by empire-builders."

Speak white
it is so beautiful to hear you
talk about Paradise Lost
or about the charming and anonymous profiles that tremble in
the sonnets of Shakespeare

We are an uncultivated and stuttering people
But we are not deaf to the genius of a language
speak with the accent of Milton and Byron and Shelley and
Keats

speak white
and forgive us for only having as a response
the harsh chants of our ancestors
and the sadness of Nelligan

. . .speak white and loud
so that we will hear you
from Saint-Henri to Saint-Dominique
yes what an admirable language
to hire
to give orders
to fix the hour of death at work
and the pause that refreshes
and revives the dollar

. . .it's a rich language
to buy
but also to sell oneself
but to sell oneself to the loss of
one's soul
but to sell oneself.

There is, of course, more, but you get the general thrust of it.

Mr. Besner asserts the references made to Shakespeare et al "are tributes to the excellence of their language." Thus, the lines:

we aren't a very clever people
but very able to appreciate
all the importance of crumpets
or of the Boston Tea Party.

are really nothing but a sincere tribute to English cooking and the American revolution.

But Mr. Besner is right about one thing: "Speak White" has been around for a long time, at least since 1969. As dated as it was at its writing, it is even more dated — and more inflammatory — in 1978, the year of Bill 101. It is, if nothing else, a provocative, unjustified piece of mischief, calculated, in my opinion, to encourage hatred, ridicule and contempt of the English language, and those who speak it.

It should be clear — even to Mr. Besner — that I have no objection to Michele Lalonde's poem, as little as I think of it, or to its being screamed from the rooftops of every coffee house in Montreal, so long as listening is not obligatory.

What is apparently unclear to Mr. Besner is that I have a growing uneasiness and dismay over the machinations of the Parti Quebecois government. In that respect, the poem does not matter so much as the occasion of its revival, and the sponsors of the occasion.

Mr. Besner doubtless finds much that is admirable in such a government. It is my own opinion that it is the most dangerous government ever elected in the country, and my further opinion that it is incubating sentiment in Quebec that I can best define as racist.

"Secondly," writes Mr. Besner, "Dalton Camp goes on to say that the reading of the poem sparked off a ten-minute standing ovation. Bullroar!"

Bullroar indeed. Dalton Camp said no such thing; he did not even say that Parti Quebecois Justice Minister Marc-André Bédard joined in the ovation by applauding with his hands held over his head, so great was his enthusiasm.

23 February 1979

This was the week I found myself in agreement with Marc Lalonde, something I am sure will unsettle both of us, as well as defy the established laws of probability.

It happened this way. The premier of Quebec, who appears to have come down with something, described those in his province who are federalists as "foreigners." And furthermore, "lackeys." The federal justice minister responded by categorizing Lévesque's remarks as having "almost racist implications."

Why "almost?" But rather than seem captious, let us say that, for Marc Lalonde, "almost racist" is close enough.

Some months ago — last August, more precisely — I found myself upon a sea of troubles for suggesting that the reading of a poem, called "Speak White," to a captive audience at an official fête staged by the government of Quebec, was an example of racism.

The trouble with "Speak White" as poetry is that it can mean damn near anything, as I learned. There are those who claim it is a poetic defence of all the downtrodden — in all the world. Others, whose intellects and ideologies are not so finely tuned, thought as I did that it invited resentment and encouraged hostility against those who spoke English — "an admirable language. . . to fix the hour of death," as the poet put it.

Someone else maintained that while the poem might not be racist — perhaps only almost racist — the time and place chosen by the Parti Quebecois government for resurrecting it was singularly inappropriate. What could they, the authors of Bill 101, have had in mind?

As the result of formal complaint, I found myself and the offending column brought before the Ontario Press Council, and, while tried in absentia (the principle of habeas corpus being outside the writ of the Press Council), I got the impression that I escaped rebuke only to provide example of the right of anyone to produce eccentric opinion, and the *Toronto Star* to circulate it. To say that I was gratified, or relieved, by this dispensation, would be putting it too strongly.

But, as the premier of Quebec would say, vive quelque chose.

I think it possible that even Mao Tse-tung could have read "Speak White" and found it inspiring of revolutionary thought; similarly, it is possible for some to read *The Merchant of Venice* and find it an inspired tract against usury; on the other hand, it has been argued that it also inspires anti-semitism. All readers of *Oliver Twist* recognize Fagin as a Jew, and some find his character reinforces their prejudices.

It is appropriate, then, that the genesis of Lévesque's "foreigners" remark is from a Quebecois folksinger of whom, I have no doubt, it will be said that his balladry is intended only to comfort those who suffer from ring around the collar.

It is chilling, however, to realize that when the premier of Quebec describes tens of thousands of those whom he governs, and who disagree with him, as being "for all intents and purposes, even if they are unaware of it, 'foreigners' " he means it.

We are coming down to refinements of ethnic purity, for lack of which people elsewhere in history have been ostracized, discriminated against, or stoned in the streets. The separatist rhetoric now becomes menacing, evolving from pledges to purify the political system into threats to deprive impure dissenters of their citizenship.

All the same, it has perhaps been a useful exchange. While nothing said has been much of a surprise to me, it might wake up others who have been so lulled by the haze of charisma that surrounds the first minister of Quebec as not to have noticed that he is speaking now in the accents of a bully.

6 May 1980

Just as the Ontario legislature was launched upon a lengthy debate — seventy speakers, seventy! — dealing with a resolution urging Quebeckers to vote "no" in the referendum, a counter-group emerged elsewhere in Toronto, calling upon politicians outside of Quebec to adopt a more constructive attitude towards a "yes" vote, if there is one.

Melville Watkins, who was last seen teaching in the Department of Political Economy at the University of Toronto, emerged as the spokesperson for the group, which included Margaret Atwood and Margaret Laurence, among others. For those with short memories, I will remind them that Professor Watkins was once the designated thorn in the side of the NDP, the leader of the self-described Waffle Movement, which had to do with ultra-economic nationalism. He was also once appointed chairman of a task force by then Prime Minister Lester Pearson, a politician who was willing to try anything in the interest of meaningful dialogue, to enquire into American control of Canadian industry and the evils thereof.

I appear to have no evidence in my normally adequate files to shed light on whatever became of the Task Force although, dimly, I recall the production of a Watkins Report which, I suspect, Lester Pearson quickly buried somewhere beneath the sod on Parliament Hill. But all this, I hasten to add, is only by way of saying that I've invariably found Watkins an engaging and stimulating fellow, even though occasionally unnerving.

So saying, I welcome his re-emergence and, I suppose, what he has come out of the cloister to say had to be said by someone, sooner or later, the laws of probability not having been repealed at Massey College. It is true that the firm resistance among politicians in the rest of Canada to the thought of negotiating sovereignty-association with the province of Quebec is sufficiently monolithic as to suggest a conspiracy. When, if ever, has there been such perfect accord among so many federal and provincial Grits, Tories and social democrats as on this issue?

But the resistance is real. Watkins and his group may be the innocent vanguard of a measurable body of public opinion which has been heard to say often enough that "if Quebec wants to go, then let them go." Supposedly, the details would be unimportant and could all be worked out by whomever could be found to volunteer the time. Against the view, however, is a sizeable body of opinion unwilling and unable to accommodate those who would destroy Canada.

To suggest that we should now be discussing how best to carve up the remains of the country, in anticipation of having to do so, seems ludicrous. What we do know is that if such is ever to be done, we will require a whole new generation of politicians, since none of those we have now have either the talent for it or the inclination. Obviously, so complete a transfusion will take some time.

Mel Watkins, whose IQ is sufficiently large as to tempt one to nationalize it, must know better. I suspect his outburst is largely a manifestation of his habitual discomfort in the face of so much agreement: since so many of us think more or less alike, a lot of us must be more or less wrong.

Maybe so, but not on this matter. After all, it was the good professor himself who wrote on a theme closely bearing upon our present dilemmas. According to Watkins: "It would be criminal to stand idly by applauding the decline of the nation-state. But it would be equally derelict to imagine that nationalism can be an adequate answer to our present discontents. The compelling need for the future is not for national societies in a world community — desirable though such a social system would be today — but rather for a world society fit for a global village."

And then Watkins quotes Camus: "To feel one's attachment to a certain region, one's love for a certain group of men, to know there is always a spot where one's heart will feel at peace — these are many certainties for a single human life. And yet this is not enough."

Right on, Mel! Right on, Albert!

So why this haste to dismantle a nation-state of two and more nations which, given the opportunity for further ingenuity, would make an ideal society for tomorrow's global village? Surely, not in the interest of a more narrow nationalism.

An Open Letter to the Premiers of the Provinces of Canada:

May it please your illustrious selves: Your humble correspondent — being merely a simple citizen, unworthy taxpayer, and lowly scribe — makes bold to offer two suggestions as to the conduct of your business on the occasion of the forthcoming First Ministers' Conference to be held in that abandoned railway station in Ottawa, Ontario. Like many another Canadian, I have circled the dates of 8-12 September on my calendar, these being the days which will celebrate your gracious presences in the nation's capital, and days which I, for one, await with bated breath, even while, at the same time, holding it.

First, may I suggest a change of venue? If you are, as the thunder rolling out of Winnipeg after your last get-together indicates, coming to Ottawa to receive the surrender of the federal government, why meet in the station? How about meeting in a railway car?

You will recall, being historians, that after World War I, the surrender ceremonies were held in a railway car, drawn up in a siding at Compiègne, France. Talk about photo opportunities, eminences; many of the prints are still in circulation!

Indeed, the World War I railway car is still there, and I need not press upon you the value of a similar car located on a siding alongside the Rideau Canal, which would, once the formalities were complete and the documents signed, become an instant historic sight — the last railway car in Canada. Ottawa would thus become one of the great museums in the world, containing within its precincts such relics as the House of Commons, the Senate, the old Department of National Revenue, Michael Pitfield's chair and — of course — the railway car. With a tug of the forelock and a deep bow, exalted ones, I trust you will find within your hearts the compassion at least to do for tourism what you could not do for Canada — give it a little boost.

I can remember earlier days and other federal-provincial conferences, as they used to call them, when your short-sighted, naïve predecessors used to meet. With profound respect, may I say how different those occasions were from those which now crowd upon us. You might find it hard to believe — and I wish not to exhaust your credulity — but back in those days we used to hear premiers, like Joe Smallwood from Newfoundland, take up all their time praising the government of Canada. Imagine!

And I would say to the mighty and glorious premier of British Columbia — and long may he reign over us — that his daddy would come to these things and urge the federal government to do more to help Maritimers and other needy folk. I even remember one meeting at which Premiers Les Frost of Ontario and Tommy Douglas of

Saskatchewan went out of their way to support a federal proposal for giving a few million extra dollars to the Atlantic Provinces.

Then there was Duplessis from Quebec — ole' Maurice — who always used to play the conference heavy. But he had a hard job much of the time keeping a straight face, and most of us, except the Liberals, knew him for what he was — a pussycat, and a Canadian one.

Of course, since then, a lot of us have struck it rich and I suppose it's only natural a man's view of things will change according to what he has in his pocket, or at the bank, offshore, or under the ground. There's no room left nowadays for sentiment, national or otherwise, and your esteemed selves and your advisors have a clear and noble duty to take all you can get.

Finally, los magníficos, if you don't like my idea of the railway car, and want to postpone the surrender ceremonies for another day, I suggest you consider a second idea of mine, which you may be merciful enough to give brief thought to sometime over lunch between the foie gras and the gâteaux forestierre.

I have in mind those long-winded opening statements, which, through no fault of your impeccable selves, have come to sound, to ordinary mortals such as the Canadian people, self-serving, redundant and familiar. This time, why not — just for the hell of it — each of you make an opening statement about the kind of Canada we've got, and what's best about it, and the new, improved Canada you'd like to see in the future, long after you've all taken your richly deserved pensions?

I trust, o great ones, that none of the above will be considered other than the most respectful advice from a faithful, adoring, abject subject, and a tv fan of each and every one of you.

18 November 1980

It is winterset: acid snow falls at the window and the Grey Cup is at hand. Torontonians, who no longer have all the luck, at least have the Big Game and, even as this is written from a distant Canadian outport, thousands of Albertans are descending upon the Queen City, come to cheer on their beloved Eskimaux against the foe from Hamilton. They have come to the right place: Toronto needs the money.

How often have we heard the annual oration on the theme of the miraculous healing powers of football as demonstrated by the therapeutic value of the Grey Cup to the cause of National Unity? It is just one more contribution for which we have America to thank — a playing field full of Yankee gladiators uniting Canadians each November in brotherly love. To tell the truth, I have had doubts as to the validity of this, since the more often of late Edmonton has won Earl Grey's silver, the more the country has seemed to fall apart. Could there be some link between the ascendant West's superior recruitment of American fugitives from the NFL and the decline of western enthusiasm for eastern politicians?

We shall have all these theorems tested, if not sorely tried, when Alberta comes to Toronto to play Hamilton. If football be the balm for National Unity, we will see if its unguent powers can sluice the way for a reunion of Premier Peter Lougheed and Premier Bill Davis. Will they sit together at the game, as Lougheed sat with Manitoba's Sterling Lyon for the western play-off? And if they do, who will serve as interpreter?

But there's more. Will the prime minister be returned from Yemen in time for the kick-off and — if you were Jake Gaudaur and setting the table for this feast of harmony — where would you seat Trudeau? Between Lougheed and Davis? Or Davis — host premier — in the centre, with the prime minister safely on his right? Surely no other sporting event on earth is attended by such wracking problems.

The questions extend beyond protocol and the subtleties of diplomacy to hard-ball politics. One suspects that if the prime minister can find another Middle East country to visit, he will flee there, avoiding the Grey Cup, pleading the national interest and the requirements of the Third World. Still, there is the real world, too, at Exhibition Stadium, and Canadians everywhere await another injection of National Unity, a serum on which the prime minister has claimed the patent.

It could be, at the last minute, that Lougheed himself may ask for a refund on his ticket. He has, after all, seen a lot of football games, and unlike others in the upper echelons of politics, actually played in a number of them. But the premier of Alberta is only human, recent reports to the contrary, and the prospect of being a prominent spectator at yet another humiliation of Ontario would be alluring enough even to fetch him from a sick bed. Add to that the not-so-marginal benefit of watching Davis watching Edmonton walloping the relics of eastern football predominance, and you have, for a Tory like Lougheed, an irresistible reason to attend — private incentive.

When it's over (Edmonton 30, Hamilton 10)*, we can measure the rise in National Unity in the body politic. It might be that the premier of Ontario will emerge from the dressing room to say, "Peter and I," (Bill always calls Lougheed "Peter") "have talked things over and we've agreed to forget this past season, the ecstasies of victory and the

*Actually, Edmonton 30, Hamilton 0

agonies of defeat, and one thing and another, and start looking ahead to next season and the rebuilding job we have to do for Team Canada."

It could also be that the prime minister will emerge arm-in-arm with both Davis and Lougheed, saying, as they sally forth into Toronto the Good, "I simply told the first ministers at half-time that if those guys from Edmonton can play as a team, so can I. The universe is unfolding the only way it can in a country like this. We've just seen some guys from the United States playing for a trophy donated by a British nobleman for the football championship of Canada. I hope all Canadians will recognize what a great country this is."

Following that, Canadians will rush out into the winter night and light bonfires to celebrate National Unity at its apogee.

It could happen, but don't bet on it. Bet Edmonton.

24 November 1980

In the decade of the seventies, there were a number of sure-fire ways of getting on television, especially if you were an American, although Canadians too got into the act. One could occupy the dean's office, ransack his files and hurl epithets from the windows; one could also throw computers out the window, a Canadian innovation; or one might immolate one's draft card, call policemen pigs, or smoke pot in public. One could also throw pies at politicians, or streak.

Producers of public affairs programs used to dispatch film crews to the campus — any would do — to obtain visual evidence of the presence of restless students. They never failed in their mission. Once the camera had been set up, a crowd would gather; you asked a few probing questions, got a few salty answers, and, before your eyes, the crowd would begin to demonstrate. You then had enough verisimilitude to confirm the most apocalyptic of commentaries from studio sociologists and political scientists.

The campus demonstrations in America were understandable, if not always supportable. There was, after all, the war in Vietnam and the draft. In Canada, where there was neither, the demonstrations did not lack for a commensurate zeal. Happily, a deadly hush has long since fallen on academia.

But the needs of television and radio, as with the restless search for celebrity among those who know they will never be media stars, unless they become media events, remain unquenched. And now Canadians have struck the mother lode — at least enough potential sound and film to meet the needs of the beginnings of the decade; western separatism, the first truly all-Canadian media fix!

79

Like that old pejorative chestnut, "unilateral patriation," western separatism pleads for definition. If you were tracking it down, how long would you spend searching for it in Manitoba? Are they heading for the exits in Brandon and The Pas? And if not there, what of Saskatchewan? True, we do know of two renegade Tories who have recently declared they would rather have their potash legislation laid down in Fargo, North Dakota; but there are probably as many cases of yellow fever in Saskatchewan as there are folks stricken with separatism.

So, if western separatism is to be found, we must search Alberta and British Columbia. One must extend credulity to its limits to imagine the merger of these two western provinces into one glorious independent nation. (Because of the prevalence of warm chinooks in one and warm rain in the other, they might call the new nation Baked Alaska.) Still, I overheard this morning the warning of a pending television "special" on western separatism being worked up by one of the networks.

I doubt British Columbia is ready for separation, or ever would be. Its premier, Bill Bennett, a fellow who wouldn't tell you what time it was without first having the unanimous consent of the provinces, took a very firm position against separatism during the Quebec referendum, travelling the distance to Montreal to do it. What's sauce for Quebecois ought to be the same for British Columbians: you can include B.C. out of the movement.

Even though one of Bennett's own ministers has lately given the cause limp endorsement, you can be secure in the knowledge, gathered from historic example, that cabinet ministers in British Columbia have been found guilty of everything but profundity.

By such painstaking deductions, we are left with the evidence that western separatism is a wholly-owned and operated Alberta enterprise. To admit to it, however, diminishes the prospect, and the audience, for hair-raising accounts of hordes of western separatists pounding on the doors of the Canadian federation.

Of course, there was the big western separatist rally in Edmonton last week — three thousand out to hear the evangelical intonations of one man who finally made it on the national networks. The rally was the major Canadian news event of the weekend. Hell, where I come from we get better crowds than that for bingo.

2 December 1980

The Canada West Foundation recently sponsored a three-day conference in Banff, Alberta, at which some two hundred delegates were invited to consider western options and alternatives to constitutional change. The conference can only be described as the greatest man-made disaster since the Mississauga derailment.

The deliberations began, as is customary, with all present sitting down to a banquet, after which the organizers served up to the delegates the chairman of Canada West, Arthur Child, otherwise the president of Burns Foods Limited, a Calgary firm not previously noted for flavouring its after-dinner treats with tabasco. Anyway, Mr.Child proved too hot for the tastes of some as he delivered an encyclopaedic fulmination against the federal government, very nearly restoring it to favour by doing so.

When the chairman declared that "Western Canadians are opposed to the entrenchment of language rights in the constitution," audible sounds of dissent, or disbelief, could be heard in the room. A few brave souls struggled to their feet and, leaning into gusts from the podium, walked out, taking the first Cadillac back to Calgary. From there on, the conference gathered the downhill momentum appropriate to winter weekends at Banff.

The Canada West Foundation has been respectably known as a non-political research organization devoted to promoting and publicizing western Canadian interests. It is financially assisted by all four provincial governments in the region and by donations from the private sector. It is common knowledge that the foundation has all the money it needs; it is becoming less certain it has all its marbles.

For example, Canada West has embarked upon an advertising campaign urging readers to clip coupons from the ads and send them to Margaret Thatcher, Britain's prime minister. The coupons beseech Mrs. Thatcher to defy the government of Canada by returning the British North America Act without amendment, a prayer certain to go unanswered unless the Rt. Hon. lady has become as unhinged as the members of the executive council of Canada West appear to be.

Let's see now: are the citizens of Canada being implored to ask of the prime minister of Britain that she withhold the requests of the government of Canada for constitutional amendment because the Canada West Foundation is opposed to the entrenchment of language rights? And if so, would it be okay if a similar campaign were mounted by some other foundation urging Mrs. Thatcher to do the opposite? And ought the question then be resolved, one way or another, according to which side sent in the most coupons?

While pondering that, consider the further recommendation of Canada West, unveiled at its Banff conference, calling for the election of a "constituent council," which would be given a year to write a new constitution. Then, and only then, would Mrs. Thatcher be invited to send the BNA Act home for revision. The idea sounds as though it were arrived at in committee; one made up of Joe Clark, Claude Ryan, Pepin-Robarts, and culled from the speeches of John Diefenbaker. All of whom, at least, have romanced the notion of a constituent assembly on the constitution, but it still remains one of those rare solutions of which it can be said that its greatest appeal is that it hasn't been tried since 1776, in another jurisdiction.

The problem with any such constitutent assembly — unless it were desperately rigged as to representation — is that the regional biases and the numbers will produce either a result similar to the objectionable one now before us, or one much worse. The creation of yet another elected body to settle our national differences will probably not be any wiser than those we have, including the federal House, the Senate, and the legislatures, none of which have proven to be founts of wisdom. As the Canada West Foundation has conclusively proved, the electorate doesn't always provide the best people to produce the best answers for us, but money doesn't either.

23 December 1980

This being the Holiday Season, it might be as good a time as any to explain my unqualified support of the federal government's initiative to amend and patriate the Canadian constitution. It is, after all, a time of year when most of us are presumably full of goodwill and perhaps even patience.

The main reason, perhaps even the only one (I believe the prime minister to be right on this issue, and wish him well), relates directly to the proposal to entrench minority language educational rights — French and English — in the constitution (with the caveat "where numbers warrant"). I support this less in the interest of any English minority and more in that of the French minority.

Such a right, entrenched in the federal constitution, extends and broadens the basic rights of all francophones. Heretofore, language educational rights being the presumed preserve of the provinces, anyone born and raised in the province of Quebec, for example, grew up in the knowledge that entitlement to an education in one's own tongue was restricted to within provincial boundaries. Since Canada itself offered no such entitlement, other than by favour, it is not remarkable that generations of French Canadians in Quebec thought of their province as the sole guarantor of their language and culture, and of Canada as a potential menace to it.

It explains the political efficacy of such slogans as "maîtres chez nous," or "égalité ou independance," even as it explains the growth of separatism itself. Certainly it explains why generations of competing provincial politicians in Quebec sought to limit the federal presence and to minimize its roles in Quebec, just as they sought to aggrandize the role of the provincial government. So that we reached, by 1976 if not before, the absurdity in francophone Canada by which provincial members were deemed to speak for Quebec while federal members spoke only for Ottawa.

The entrenchment of minority language educational rights would mean that future generations in Quebec could look to the Canadian constitution as being the ultimate guarantor and protector of their language. It would mean that Canada would provide them not only with the rights to their language in education, but with considerably expanded opportunities as Canadian citizens.

It is true that some of the premiers more or less agree with entrenchment; it is obvious the premier of Quebec does not. But it is inconceivable, unless the constitution were first turned upside down with regard to the distribution of powers, that any Quebec premier would ever agree to such an amendment. The fact that the government of Quebec disagrees, however, is no more significant than the fact that the Liberal federal members, representing every constituency in the province save one, are in almost unanimous support of the amendment.

Further, it is unlikely we will have this unusual combination of factors — a francophone prime minister with overwhelming support in Quebec — which is another way of saying that so sensitive an issue could never be resolved by an anglophone prime minister or anyone else who had any less francophone support.

Thus, those who maintain, as some premiers have done, that they support the entrenchment of language rights but want unanimity, or want to go back to the bargaining table, or would wait until after patriation, are, for whatever reason, including that of self-interest, simply being unrealistic.

I suspect the opposition to entrenchment of some anglophone premiers is helpful to the issue, just as the support of Premiers Davis and Hatfield is helpful to it. If language rights were to be entrenched in the constitution with the unanimous approval of the anglophone premiers and the singular dissent of the premier of Quebec, many might draw back from such a confrontation. It is better, for historic and other reasons, that this be done without the appearance of English Canada being ranged against the province of Quebec on a matter of particular sensitivity to French Canada.

There are those, like Premier Blakeney of Saskatchewan, who have lately seemed supportive of the language provisions in the Charter of Rights. But he is against the entrenchment of some other rights. Again, it would not have been wise for the federal government to isolate language rights as the only amendment; that would have been even more inflammatory. And those of us who see little danger in a constitution which guarantees, among other things, "freedom of thought, belief, opinion and expression," are consoled by the evidence of arguments from lawyers on both sides: it will ever be thus.

It seems to me that all the circumstances are as ideal as they will ever be for constitutional change; should we not seize the opportunity now, it will not soon come again.

14 January 1981

Vancouver

Out here, which is as far west in this country as a man can go without getting his feet wet, a visitor is advised not to take western separatism lightly.

As for western alienation, it is as visible as the lights on Grouse Mountain on a clear night. It is also audible. Mention Ottawa, the constitutional proposals, or P.E. Trudeau, and the air becomes filled with bellows of rage, mentions of the Deity and multiple imprecations. To the east, in neighbouring Alberta, bumper stickers express a penultimate opinion on the prime minister: "He Goes or We Go."

It is a sentiment that is sweeping — has swept — western Canada. You would need to be deaf not to hear it, and simply dumb not to believe its conviction. But Trudeau is merely the arch-villain, not the only one. Among the larger, if lesser, luminaries in black hats are Ottawa bureaucrats, federal apologists (such as I) and Central Canada. In other words, when the prime minister takes his leave of politics, it will help matters some. The depopulation of Ontario would help even more, and if the few public defenders of the proposed constitutional revisions were strangled in their beds, peace would be restored in the land, even though we might need to rename it.

Seen from this side of the mountains, there is a new view of Canada, a vision inspired by the growing imbalance between resource wealth and population. Where the wealth is found, the numbers are still few; where the numbers are found, so too are the looters, carpet-baggers and welfare indolents. And since democracy is the rule of numbers, the pillage of the west seems certain.

There is considerably more than a brooding suspicion that what Central Canada wants from the West, now hostage to the federal system, is ransom enough to pay for Chrysler, regional disparity and other of the incurable ailments of the declining East. Since the economic ascendency of western Canada has left the rest of the country so far behind, even that dear old Canadian principle of equalization no longer looks like a modest federal transfer payment but resembles instead daylight robbery. But even before the constitutional package, which proposes to entrench the principle of equalization, British Columbians sensed the danger posed by elementary Canadian democracy when all those Ontario voters elected the party (Liberal) which promised them western energy at the cheapest price.

The mistrust and resentments have been earned, even though the recital of them does not help resolve the problems. Unless goodwill and trust are restored, the West will remain as implacable as Ottawa has been intransigent, and I would have to say that while western mistrust of the East is considerable, it is not so excessive as eastern ignorance of the West. Indeed, in this presumed age of communications, the absolute void in understanding is a staggering achievement, even for Canadians.

Having endured the slights, taunts and insults of some hundred Vancouverites, assembled in the Vancouver Club under the guise of marking the birthday of Sir John A. Macdonald, I have emerged bloodied but unbowed — and also chastened. Travel is broadening, and it is unfortunate that the prime minister, among others, has chosen to broaden his experience by travelling in the opposite direction from his most dire responsibilities. At least, it seemed an absurdity to me, that while defending his constitutional proposals in the face of measurable hostility and flying hard rolls, he should be in Senegal studying North-South relations and I should be directly experiencing east-west relations, Canadian style.

Anyway, because of the bibulous nature of the audience — the evening being properly observed in Sir John's memory — I escaped alive. And I continue to hope for patriation, entrenchment and the early retirement of the prime minister. But yes, the fears and grievances of the West are genuine; there is as much merit in their argument as there is heat.

What they fear, in these western reaches, is the tyranny of the majority, a feeling not unknown to the framers of our constitution and one originally recognized in the interests of Quebec and Prince Edward Island, among others. Westerners are concerned that the constitution is again being repaired, as it originally was framed, without their being present or represented. Considering this, the direful results of the last election and the further provocation of the federal budget of Allan MacEachen, easterners will need more than their numbers to assure the survival of unity and equity in the Canadian democracy. As to this, more later.

The British, as Paul Revere once said, are coming. We seem to be inundated these days with lords and knights of the empire — there is the good Sir Francis Pym,* the noble Sir Anthony Kershaw, the indomitable Sir John Ford, and, of course, m'Lord Morris. Any day now, we should hear from Sir Brian Botany. To invert a familiar euphemism, if diplomacy be war by other means, we are apparently at war with Britain.

There is a tendency in Canada, especially in neo-colonial circles, to be awed, if not cowed, by any expression of opinion rendered in the Queen's perfect English by a man whose surname is decorated with a title. But not all the lords and knights of the realm earned their titles on merit; in fact, the titled meritocracy is of modest size compared with the titled mediocrity, which is considerable.

In Britain, it is not necessary to slay a dragon to earn a knighthood. You can (a) buy a title; (b) acquire one along with a Golden Handshake; (c) be given one as compensation for proven incompetence; or (d) get one by being the crony of a prime minister (Jimmy Goldsmith comes to mind).

Harold Laski used to say that approximately half the members of the House of Lords got there because they were public disasters and the other half because their fathers were dead. And while I have frequently departed from the teachings of Professor Laski, I have learned he was not always wrong. Anyway, the purpose of this seeming digression is to remind us that the British have a monopoly only on political titles; they have none on political judgment.

But never mind the political judgment of Sir John — after all, Fords always have a better idea, even unto Commonwealth relations — or of Sir Anthony, who has become the first Briton since Queen Victoria to take his duty to Canada seriously; I am transfixed by Lord Morris.

In a fit of prescience, his Lordship has declared that the Canadian government's resolution "hasn't a prayer" of being approved by the House of Lords. He must be right because Sir Anthony, weighing the question while visiting Edmonton, said he was inclined to think so, too.

This ought to be instructive to Canadians who are uncertain as to the nature and limits of their national sovereignty; under present conditions, it is perceived by some, at least, to be limited and unnatural.

The government and Parliament of Canada cannot, the argument runs, determine what is to be done about the constitution. Instead, the backbenchers at Westminster, according to Sir Anthony Kershaw,

An irate reader has pointed out that Francis Pym has not received a knighthood—yet.

have a prior duty and responsibility to "adjudicate" the matter. And even then, assuming a benevolent adjudication, the will of the Canadian Parliament can be thwarted in, of all places, the British House of Lords.

Our national sovereignty is thus so limited as to be laughable.

That this is of consolation to the neo-colonial Canadian mind is understandable. It truly believes the British should adjudicate in this issue, just as it naturally assumes the innate superiority of those who have titles.

In such a world of perfect symmetry, the Canadian Parliament becomes merely the eleventh of Canada's legislatures, not the ultimate one, a notion, incidentally, firmly embedded in the Kershaw Report.

So far, this great, trans-oceanic constitutional debate has been instructive and, as well, highly entertaining. The most merciful resolution to it would come with a decision upholding the Canadian government by the Supreme Court of Canada, domestic adjudication which might even influence the House of Lords. It seems the most merciful, if only because the alternatives appear bleak indeed.

Meanwhile, it is much too early to look for damage to our relations with Britain. P.E. Trudeau is not the first prime minister of Canada to create an uproar in British political circles, any more than the British high commissioner is the first diplomat in Ottawa to suffer from an excess of zeal.

Somehow, this too will be endured and at negligible risk to the monarchy or the Commonwealth connection. Stanley Baldwin once advised his reluctant parliamentary supporters to vote for women's suffrage, "if not in a spirit of enthusiasm, then in one of utter resignation."

Sooner or later, it will likely come to that; surely the country which once ruled the waves will never waive the rules?

Parental Guidance Recommended

7 June 1979

During his winning election campaign, our new prime minister, C.J. Clark, used to put down his Liberal hecklers by directing them to the nearest telephone booth where, he would say, they could hold a meeting of all those who wanted to re-elect a Trudeau government.

The telephone booth has since been dismantled, but I suggest hammering it up again so as to have a suitable meeting place for all those who voted Conservative on election day to express their positive enthusiasm for the Tory platform. Indeed, if anyone got votes purely for the allure of a platform, it was the Rhinoceros Party.

More than that: so far as the Tory platform was concerned, the editorial pages of a nearly universal anti-Trudeau and pro-Tory press declared a moratorium during the campaign on attempting any critical analysis of Conservative policy intentions. The velvet glove glued to every editorial fist remained stuck even when the Tory leader, in mid-campaign, divulged his plan to move the Canadian embassy to Jerusalem. Even though everyone else, notably the reporters, thought the declaration astonishing, the moulders and shapers of national thought on the editorial pages remained eerily silent.

Well, with the election over and — That Man having departed in his vintage Mercedes — mission accomplished, one notices a stirring in the ivory towers along media row. You can hear the clearing of throats and the rattling of quill pens. While it is always possible, though not likely, that Clark's leap into Middle East politics was initially read as election strategy rather than foreign policy, it is now clear that he really meant it. Since he does mean it, and there is much to be said against it, we are now at last going to have the issue discussed, at least in the media. (All those who truly believed that those editorials were serious which pronounced election campaigns to be the supreme moment for serious public discussion of serious public issues may now proceed to another telephone booth.)

But yes, the prime minister intends to do what he proposed he would do when he was running for office. And since the moratorium has been lifted, some, though not all, may speak up on the subject.

To begin with, the proposal to relocate the Canadian embassy was not agreed-upon party policy. There is not much wrong with the prevailing opinion that the genesis of the Jerusalem move was the close race in the Toronto riding of St. Paul's and that the notion was pressed upon Clark by his candidate there, Ron Atkey, who believed he needed it to win. The decision to go with it was not taken by the party, the caucus, or the campaign committee, but by Clark, flying at thirty-five thousand feet in his DC-9. When the leader subsequently went public on the matter — in, of course, Toronto — his Tory troops in Ottawa and elsewhere were as surprised as was, say, the Canadian ambassador in far-off Jeddah.

The prime minister's present posture is one of a curious defiance. Plainly, his knowledge of foreign policy is limited. But he is not, he assures us, going to waste time hearing the advice of those who might know more than he — in fact, are certain to know more. Thus: ". . . matters that have been part of party policy in the election campaign. . . these questions are now beyond discussion as to their appropriateness, and what we will be seeking from the public service will be indications as to how we accomplish what we have undertaken to do."

So saith the prime minister. But, saith one of his constituents, that is a hell of a way to run a government. Never mind the incontestable fact that the particular matter — that of moving the embassy — is not, and never was, party policy (unless we revert to instant tribalism to say that whatever he says, we all will say). But pay closer attention to this peremptory dismissal of the accumulated experience, knowledge, wisdom and expertise of the Department of External Affairs, a department of government which has brought international distinction, credit and deserved respect to Canada. What Clark is saying is that whatever the department's wisdom might be, he doesn't want to hear it.

But never mind. We are soon to become troublemakers in the world's most dangerously troublesome area, and to provoke the sensibilities of literally millions who have, historically, trusted us for our good offices. Yet it will, however, bring the boys back home from their last peacekeeping mission abroad.

Pity Flora MacDonald, who promised so much in her new portfolio as minister of our most distinguished department. Having offended a dozen nations, previously our friends, and having appalled our traditional allies, and — yes — given new incentive to fanaticism, Miss MacDonald's debut as foreign minister will be marked more by its notoriety than its promise, and she will be as welcome in the company of her as yet unknown opposite numbers as Madame Pompadour would be at an annual meeting of the Synod. And just as the prime minister crawls out on that limb, he drags us all along with him. It seems a high price for St. Paul's.

22 June 1979

No one could have been surprised to read the rebuttal from E.A. Goodman to my column a fortnight ago in which I took issue with the prime minister, C.J. Clark, over the issue of moving the Canadian embassy in Israel from Tel Aviv to Jerusalem. While Eddie Goodman and I have been friends for many years, we have as often been in disagreement over political matters as we have been in accord. It is a tribute to Goodman's capacity for friendship, as well as to his fundamental civility, that our relationship has never been impaired merely because we did not see alike.

For example, Goodman and I disagreed, loudly, on the issue of lodging American nuclear weapons on Canadian soil; he wanted them here and I did not. As a result, I supported the prime minister, John Diefenbaker, on the issue, and in the campaign of 1963, contrary-minded, Mr. Goodman publicly resigned his office on the party's national executive and sat out the campaign.

Later on, as a direct consequence, avenging Ontario Tories voted Goodman off the provincial party executive — to my pronounced dismay and outrage. He spent some time, after that, living in the splendour of involuntary exile in Forest Hill, Toronto. Thus, when he began his critique of my position on the Jerusalem issue, and of my "writing from the splendour of self-imposed exile" somewhere in New Brunswick, I'm sure he did so as one exile speaking to another, knowing, from experience, how easy it is to endure.

It is one of Goodman's positively endearing qualities, recognized and respected by his friends, that he cares passionately about a wide range of political issues and, to his credit, is a persistent, resourceful, persuasive advocate of them. You could not have a better man on your side, whether in the boardroom, the back room, a back alley, or in court.

But if you are on the other side, you should, as they say in pugilistic circles, protect yourself at all times: Goodman tends to come at you from a bewildering number of angles and not all his blows will fall above the belt. A low blow from Goodman, I need hardly say, is never deliberate, but only an accident or by-product of the intensity of his enthusiasm.

Thus, in proving me wrong about Jerusalem — that is, the decision to move the Canadian embassy there, remember — he accuses me of "weeping crocodile tears" for Flora MacDonald, the minister for external affairs, and goes on to add, "I was pleased to see Camp's concern for Miss MacDonald, as it hasn't always been shown at other crises in her career."

You see what I mean.

I am not aware, admittedly, of all the crises in the career of our mutual friend, Flora MacDonald. I can, however, recall three. One of them, when she was purged from the Tory party's national office, transpired during my first term as national president. As a consequence of the shabby treatment of Miss MacDonald, I withdrew from any contact with the national headquarters, whose national director had committed the deed, and from the national leader, Mr. Diefenbaker, who had instructed him to do so. And I maintained that posture until both of them were gone.

Which leads to the second crisis, which was Miss MacDonald's open and courageous support of the principle of leadership reappraisal and which, at great personal cost and risk, found her allied with me and a bare majority of the party. In this critical "fight for party democracy," to use Goodman's own description of it, none of us really knew where Goodman stood until, literally, the fight was over and won.

Finally — and this may be the crux of it all — in the third known crisis of Miss MacDonald's career, she contested the party leadership in 1976, against my private advice, which is and was unimportant, and without my public support, which, Goodman would admit, may even have been helpful. But while he had a special prominence as a Flora supporter, I voted for Clark and quietly canvassed for him. I doubt that Goodman would suggest, at this particular time, that this requires any apology from me.

But now, having argued to establish the primacy of his friendship with Flora MacDonald — as though it would settle the question — Mr. Goodman co-opts her true role by referring to "this decision of Clark and Miss MacDonald to move the embassy." Were I a member of the jury, I would marvel at the facility with which a gifted advocate can confuse cabinet solidarity on policy with the responsibility of those who created it. Thousands of Canadians have heard, with their own good ears, Miss MacDonald take pains to tell the CBC that the embassy move to Jerusalem was a decision taken by her leader in the campaign without her knowledge — and at even more pains to say that, even so, it was the leader's right to make policy, like instant postum, whenever it pleased him.

Surely Goodman meant to say only that it was Clark's promise to move the embassy and Miss MacDonald's obligation to fulfil it.

I have long been impressed by the obfuscatory genius of the highly trained legal mind. When I first raised the issue, publicly, of party democracy-cum-leadership reappraisal, the instant riposte from that consummate lawyer, John Diefenbaker, was that I had lost two elections in Toronto. I am positively astounded now, when, in attacking my position regarding the fitness of Clark's decision regarding the Canadian embassy in Israel, Goodman draws the same rank herring across the trail.

I lost, he points out, in Eglinton, in 1965, and in Don Valley, in 1968. But while all lawyers appear to think alike, they also embellish. Both of these ridings, Goodman continues — bringing the jury forward in their seats so as to get a good look at the smoking pistol — have, or had, "a significant 'Jewish vote.' "

Now, if you did not know Goodman as I do, you might take from that an artfully drawn implication, which would be — let us put it in lay language — that Camp's alleged unhappy political history has made of him an anti-Semite. But you see, knowing Goodman as I do — I hope — I could only believe that he would sooner be keelhauled than stoop to such a slander, but that, if it would help win his argument, he would not mind if someone else did.

We are, admittedly, a long way from treating with the substantive issue, but not nearly so far from it as Goodman will yet take us. He proceeds with his defence of Clark's election promise to move the embassy to Jerusalem by saying, "his [Camp's] appeal to the electorate in the 1968 election had not been helped by his Arab-sponsored trip to the Middle East although, certainly, we Zionists have sponsored many a similar trip."

Truthfully, you will never find in all the annals of case law — anyone from Marvin Belli to Sir Patrick Hastings — a more masterful mutation of innuendo, ambiguity and artifice.

The trouble I have with that sentence, apart from not knowing what it means, is that my appeal to the Don Valley electorate in 1968 could not have been helped or hampered by my trip to the Middle East because I didn't make the trip until 1975. But perhaps Goodman meant to say that had I gone to the Middle East in 1968, it wouldn't have helped the election. Or had I not gone then, it would have. Or it would not have helped if the electors had known in 1968 that I was going in 1975. But I did not know that it would either. Indeed, I did not make up my mind to go on this "Arab-sponsored trip" in 1975 until I personally went to Goodman as a friend and asked for his advice, which was that I should go.

If one would attempt to penetrate the armour of Eddie Goodman's concern in this matter, one must first of all admit to the integrity of his conviction. Few of us have to be, at the same time, a good Canadian and a loyal Zionist. Goodman is one who is both.

But many Canadians, including Jews, are uneasy and anxious about the potential dangers and damage to Canada's interests this singularly precipitous act could cause. There are, surely, patriots on both sides of the question. There are legitimate doubts as to the timeliness of the move, as there are honest fears of the consequences. And there are many, for one reason or another, some of them prudent and others merely timid, who will be reluctant to speak out. But it would indeed be a flawed democracy in which politicians could expect to govern in a sanctuary of silence, as Goodman himself would never allow, nor would I.

9 July 1979

Middle Quattar, Amswat

Robert L. Stanfield, appointed by Prime Minister C.J. Clark as his personal emissary, began his Middle East fact-finding tour today by holding a six-minute meeting with Emir Aram Ahmed, ruler of the Amswat Emirate. Stanfield arrived at the palace by taxi, coming directly from the airport where he touched down at noon, flying in his Canadian government-chartered Viscount.

Both the Canadian ambassador, General Percival Porteous, and the Amswat foreign minister, Abdul Abdul, failed to meet the Canadian emissary. Spokesmen for both the Embassy and the Foreign Office explained they did not know Stanfield was coming.

In an unprecedented move, the Foreign Office authorized the release of a verbatim transcript of the conversation between the Emir of Amswat and Mr. Stanfield, which an official of the ministry of information here would only characterize as "extraordinary." The transcript, as released, follows:

Emir Ahmed: "The people of my country are highly honoured that you have chosen to begin your important mission to the Middle East by visiting us."
Stanfield: "Well, we had to start somewhere, I guess."

"Before we begin our conversations, Mr. Stanfield, might we offer you coffee?"

"Nothing for me, thanks."

"After your long journey you might wish a refreshment of some kind? Is there anything you would like?"

"Maybe some water. If you have any."

"Certainly, Mr. Stanfield. May we say to our distiguished Canadian visitor that you are a long way from home?"

"Not really. We're only about 6,978 miles from Halifax. Truro would be a little further. Maybe forty miles or so."

"I trust your long journey was a comfortable one."

"Yes."

"Mr. Stanfield, it is a matter of deep regret to the Arab world that this mission of yours seems a necessary one in view of the present misunderstandings with respect to certain aspects of Canadian policy, which necessarily have worked some hardship on the longstanding friendship between ourselves and the Canadian people, for whom we have always had such great respect and admiration."

"My wife regrets it too. She's stuck with the garden and there's a lot of weeding to do, cutting back the hydrangeas, and the like."

"I understand you are an expert gardener, Mr. Stanfield."

"Oh, I wouldn't say that. I just like to putter around a bit, that's all."

"But I'm sure you do have a beautiful garden, Mr. Stanfield."

"Not really. I just put a few things out in the spring."

"Nevertheless, we appreciate the fact that a man who has given so much to his country already and is so richly entitled to enjoy his leisure would be willing to serve his government by undertaking such an important mission as one which we all hope will strengthen the bonds of Arab-Canadian friendship and understanding."

"Well, we'll have to see about that."

"We are confident, Mr. Stanfield, that in your conversations throughout the Arab world you will be impressed by the friendship of all the Arab people with Canada and their eagerness to enjoy mutually happy and increasingly profitable relationships."

"I suppose I will."

"With that united feeling of goodwill, Mr. Stanfield, you will also find great solidarity in the Arab world with respect to the highly sensitive matter of your government's policy regarding its embassy in Israel."

"I expect so."

"Mr. Stanfield, in addition to the very important matters we have already discussed, possibly there are other matters you might wish to raise?"

"No. I don't want to take any more of your time."

"We hope you will accept our apologies for our little delay in answering your telephone call from the airport."

"I wouldn't worry about that."

"We would be honoured, Mr. Stanfield, if you would join us and some of our ministers for luncheon here."

"That won't be necessary, thanks. I'll just have a bite on the plane."

"If there's anything we can do to assist you and make your visit here more comfortable and pleasant, you have only to ask."

"Well, I wonder if you could call a taxi for me."

Mr. Stanfield left Answat today, at 1:10 p.m., to continue his fact-finding mission. Asked by reporters as to the next stop on his itinerary, he said he would let them know when he got there.

Following the departure of Mr. Stanfield, the palace issued a one-sentence statement in which the Emir said, "With men of Mr. Stanfield's integrity and sincerity representing Canada, misunderstandings between that great country and the Arab world are impossible."

27 September 1979

How do you like the new Tory government so far? After nearly four months in office, the substance and style of the government of Prime Minister C.J. Clark ought to have emerged in some identifiable form. But it remains amorphous, which may be, indeed, precisely how the government wants to be seen. To answer the question, however, one would have to say of the new order in Ottawa that if it turns out to be as sound as it is methodical and as decisive as it is circumspect, then it will be a world-beater in performance.

The prime minister, of course, is a devout believer in collegial leadership and consensus. His promise to the country was that of a man who would seek conciliation and avoid confrontation. As a government, the Conservatives were pledged to defuse contentious issues and reduce the incursions of the federal government into the daily lives of Canadian citizens. Taken together, this adds up to a less visible and assertive government and one that will take a long time to make up its mind.

A high-ranking civil servant in a provincial Tory administration put it another way: "It used to be," he said, "that we could go to Ottawa and agree to disagree, and we could do that in a couple of days. But it doesn't work that way now. Even though we disagree on some issue and will always disagree, we have to keep on meeting because there's no way these guys in Ottawa are going to admit they disagree with anyone."

A provincial politician said to me that he wondered how long it would be before the prime minister realized there was such a thing as an irreconcilable difference — "even among friends" — and when the time would come, as it must for all in public life, when one must fish or cut bait. What we all know about Clark is his passion for consensus. What we have yet to find out is the direction he will take in public policy when his friends and allies are divided in their opinion and he must decide between them.

In the meantime, this has been a peripatetic government: the ministers have spent the summer visiting their provincial opposite numbers, presumably in search of improved communications. Since most of the provincial governments are Tory ones, these visits are amicable and, as every participant says afterwards with monotonous regularity, also candid. No one knows what all this candour has been about, or even why it should be considered worthy of mention. One provincial minister described the high point of a meeting with Senator Robert de Cotret as the reading of extracts from the Conservative Party's election platform, as though they were something out of the Book of Common Prayer.

What the government wants to do, I suspect, is slow down the decision-making process in the worthy name of consultation. Like all its predecessors, the Clark administration has the option of governing by legislation or by procrastination. And, as is already painfully clear, almost everything it promised to do, in the election, doesn't need doing, and in regard to the major problems of inflation and the sluggish economy, there is not very much it can do anyway.

This explains the nature and quality of public speeches now being inflicted upon lay audiences by government ministers. Though sparkling with ardour and zeal, they are stunning in their vacuity. While this lasts, it might be sensible to allow anyone willing to sit still for a speech from a cabinet minister on the subject, say, of "Whither Canada in the Age of Steam," some modest deduction from personal income tax.

It takes some time, admittedly, for a new government to settle into the seat of power. It also takes time to bring the government of Canada, as bequeathed by sixteen years of Liberalism, under some measure of control. Until both of these are at least partially achieved, it would be unreasonable to expect much more than we're getting, which are glimpses of the prime minister coming in and out of meetings and performing his daily exercises in public relations.

The last time a Tory government took office, it immediately brought in a feast of policy, providing something for nearly everyone. That was twenty-two years ago, but it will be remembered, of that government, that it soon after ran out of ideas and into trouble. History is unlikely to repeat itself in the coming of Clark to power.

In the absence of suspense, we must invent it: how long can a speech from the Throne be, on the opening of Parliament, when there is nothing in it? And how long will people be satisfied with a government whose avowed purpose is to do less and undo more than any previous government in our history?

4 October 1979

My favourite anecdote about Gordon Robertson, the upper, upper echelon federal civil servant who opted out of his job a week ago, lends a further sense of fitness to his decision to resign. When Jean Lesage and his provincial Liberal Party, to the surprise of many, swept to power in Quebec in June 1960, Robertson and an associate deputy minister were in Winnipeg, staying at the Fort Gary Hotel. When word arrived that the Union Nationale government had fallen to Lesage, Robertson and his colleague ordered up champagne to celebrate the victory.

One might ask, after the flow of history since that event: how does the wine taste now?

There was never much doubt in Tory minds, during the years of the Diefenbaker inter-regnum, that Robertson, then the deputy minister of northern affairs, was one of those who could be characterized as "a Mackenzie King Grit." But there was even less doubt that he was also a man of sensible, sound judgment with a discernible gritty integrity, no pun intended. A man of such fundamental decency and civility is hard to dislike, and any government, whatever its colour, is poorer without his services and the wisdom of his experience.

In the words of Professor Henry Higgins, the manner of Robertson's quitting his post should "set a good example" for others, including those who were appointed by the new prime minister, C.J. Clark, for the good reason, among others, that they are sympathetic to Tory policy and to the Tory cause. Robertson's letter of resignation to Clark has a touch of class and might well serve as a form letter for future resignations, down the road, when the next inevitability occurs and the government changes.

Writing to Clark, the retiring secretary to the cabinet for federal-provincial relations admitted that the result of his activities in this sensitive area of national policy had "identified me in a personal way with former policies and former governments to a degree that could embarrass your efforts to establish your own approach." Those who recall Robertson's speech at Dalhousie University a few years back, on the subject of national unity, will not argue about that.

There has been of course a battery of Tory peashooters trained upon Robertson, and pointing still at Sylvia and Bernard Ostry. The ritual masses of partisan politics call for blood sacrifice, and Ottawa seethes with rumours about the next victims to be summoned. Robertson has satisfied the lusts of the Tory hordes, but on his own terms and with his dignity intact.

He has also stuck it to Clark, in passing, with the following observation, in his letter: "I think that the most important changes you want to have now have been accomplished." No one in the national capital would disagree, but no one believes Robertson will be the last to go.

To say that the federal civil service, from top to bottom, is now a quivering, demoralized hulk of its former self would be an understatement. But apart from the reality that even good men, and women, are being obliged to end their careers for acts of loyalty to a previous régime, there are other reasons for these unsettling times. Nor is Treasury Board president Sinclair Stevens and his high-profile hatchetman's image much to blame. After all, he is merely struggling to deliver some of the goods promised in the Tory manifesto — fewer public servants spending fewer public bucks. Any government worth its mandate would do the same these days.

The truth is that even before the Clark government came to power, the middle ranks of the civil service were in the throes of a shakedown, and people with marketable skills were looking for, and finding, jobs in the private sector. They still are, and their search becomes more urgent and imperative in the face of further budget restraint, truncated programs, and abandoned plans. Almost the entire bilingual apparatus within government departments has been dismantled, a process begun under P.E. Trudeau and now with its own momentum. Believe it or not, many civil servants do not want to serve a government by doing nothing.

When all this is over, the government of Canada will have lost a considerable quotient of its expertise. It will be a body more reduced in talent than in numbers; those who remain will represent, more and more, those with limited opportunities in the private sector, while those who have departed will be those a government can least afford to lose.

But this is, apparently, what many voters earnestly want, and it will represent a genuine shift and change in the role and scope of federalism. I doubt that the reduction in numbers and quality of the public service will diminish in the slightest its established arrogance. If anything, it may increase it. Nothing could be more foreboding than the coming of a new elite of entrenched mediocrity, made up of survivors from the purge of attrition and a selected coterie of new boys whose career days will be numbered by the noble precedent of Gordon

Robertson's resignation. Meanwhile back to Mr. Stevens and the passing parade of tumbrils.

Since the lifespan of a Throne Speech is about that of a shadfly, we can consign the one which opened the thirty-first Parliament of Canada to history; no sooner said than forgotten. Still, as one with a compulsion for candour, I must commend it, for I thought more of it than did Ed Broadbent, for example.

Indeed, as an example of its kind, this one should be remembered as a model of the art of draftsmanship. It was well-constructed, smoothly polished, and with only two split infinitives. Not bad, you'd have to say, for openers.

It was also a rare sort of Throne Speech in that one could glean from it, even were one a visitor from Sri Lanka, something of the philosophy and *geist* of its sponsors, as well as their present intentions. Canadians have not been able to do that, much less anyone in the visitor's gallery, for a long time, so awesome had become the talent of preceding administrations for obfuscation.

All this, of course, is preamble and, as we know, perishable preamble at that. But it offers at least an indication that the government of Prime Minister C.J. Clark represents "a new era," to quote the speech, which may have been understatement. There is a difference in tone, style and approach, already a significant shift in priorities, and a well-gathered resolve to be faithful to the terms of its mandate.

No sooner had the promise been repeated, out of the familiar campaign rhetoric, "to demonstrate the capacity of Parliament," than was the governor of the Bank of Canada summoned to appear before a parliamentary committee to justify the bank's record thirteen per cent interest rate. That the Bank of Canada is responsible to Parliament has long been both a fiction and a convenience. The fiction allowed the government to plead innocence to complaints against the country's monetary policy, just as it allowed the bank to avoid accountability, since Parliament seldom, if ever, was given the opportunity to confront the bank's policy-makers directly on matters at issue. It has been an anomaly in more than one parliamentary democracy that, although the parliamentarians remain responsible for the consequences of central bank policy, the bank is truly responsible to no one.

Liberal administrations in the past were each devoutly establishmentarian in their faith that they would live with the fiction forever, while the previous Tory administration of John Diefenbaker was, typically, merely timid and indecisive on the issue. Clark, who has had the benefit of both these experiences, has now given Parliament, on the initiative of Herb Gray, a Liberal, the opportunity to convert the fiction of Parliament's responsibility for the bank into reality.

The governor, Gerald Bouey, will be obliged to provide a more substantive explanation for present monetary policy than that offered in the Bank's customary press releases. Public ventilation of the subject of bank interest rates will not likely change them but will be of some consolation to the many who are the hapless victims of the bank's inexplicable adumbrations. After all, in the early years — around the time of Magna Carta, say — of parliamentary government, that's what democracy promised its supporters.

What Clark has done is to permit an incursion against one of the last and most formidable bastions of autocracy and mystery. By doing so, he has fulfilled some of the promise of his government's Throne Speech almost on delivery. Given further opportunity, he may yet arrest the Parliament of Canada from the years of its decline.

Perhaps this represents the fundamental difference between the Liberal government just defeated and the Tory one now in place. It may be that the general society can be improved if we improve the quality and performance of its basic institutions. Possibly, too, if we knew more about what we are doing, we could do it better. Come to think of it, when I used to make political speeches, I used to say as much myself.

Certainly this present thrust — which rises in part from the practical lack of much else to do — towards the reform and regeneration of the old National Gas Works on Parliament Hill is worthy of effort and deserving of support. One could not imagine such priority coming from Pierre Elliott Trudeau or, for that matter, from either or any of his predecessors or successors. Liberalism operated out of elites and a bureaucracy of its own making and the longer these governed the country, the less Parliament seemed to matter. Little wonder, then, that it became so disputatious and eccentric a body.

Overnight, you might say, the coming of Clark has created some new condition. Suddenly, even the Senate is being covered by the national media. Any fair-minded observer would not call that merely remarkable; he'd have to say it's almost a miracle.

Those who might feel that a standing ovation is now in order would be wiser to keep their seats for awhile yet. The present zest for "privatization" may yet extend to destroying Petro Canada, and the bright new era in federal-provincial relations may darken early, once the central government discovers the realistic limits to a policy of consultation and conciliation. But as Icarus must have thought, as he

100

launched himself into the sunlight on his home-made wings: so far, so good.

9 January 1980

Preface to Warner Troyer, *200 Days: Joe Clark in Power* (Personal Library, 1980).

A bank manager I knew in London while I was a student at the London School of Economics once asked me what course of studies I was pursuing. I told him I was studying political science.

"Ah," he said, disdainfully, "the meanest of the sciences."

And so it is. Political scientists, I have observed, exhaust themselves in trying to find out why things happen and, once they think they know, in further attempting to organize their findings into some coherent system.

But so perverse is politics — not to mention the politicians — that systems and theories collapse under the weight of exceptions. While there is much established order in physics and chemistry, there is mostly chaos in politics, so that the very term "political science" may be a misnomer. After all, our most adroit, adept and successful practitioner of politics, Mackenzie King, was also a close student of the supernatural. He must have been on to something.

Still, human curiosity fuels the need to know, a need immediately served by journalists and, later on, by historians. For those impatient to know what happened to the Progressive Conservative minority government that came to power in Canada after the election of 22 May 1979, and was abruptly defeated in Parliament seven months later, we can only rely on the quick reflexes and resources of journalists. We will have to wait longer for the historians.

Warner Troyer sets out here to put down in an orderly manner the events that led us to the altogether unlikely federal election in the winter of 1980. It is an enterprise worthy of the considerable effort involved because so much seems to have happened in so short a time. Moreover, much of it was so contrary to commonsense expectations that even a decent chronology would be helpful. Troyer has given us more than that, helped, no doubt, by the hardnose of the professional journalist, behind which lies a wealth of knowledge of politics and of politicians. And, along with that, a discerning talent for sifting wheat from chaff.

Political prophecy — by which I mean a leap in surmise in advance of relevant data — is a mug's game. Hindsight is not only easier, but safer. Even so, it was possible to foresee trouble for the Tories even before the government fell. "The Conservatives could be in desperate trouble by next fall," wrote Geoffrey Stevens, in an early December column in the *Globe and Mail*. But not even Stevens could predict the desperate straits they would be in before Christmas 1979.

The Tories were in some trouble even before they were elected in May. The televised debate between the party leaders hurt the Conservatives more than they realized, or would admit; after that, they nervously sat on their lead, even while it was melting.

Not only did the Tories sit on their lead, they sat on their victory. After the election, one got the impression that the winners had settled into Jasper, Alberta, for a celebration of indeterminate length. Anyway, it took them four months to get over the celebration and three more to find themselves out on the hustings again.

In the meantime, I suspect, they perfected the mythology of their triumphant passage from opposition to government, the deadliest myth being that the Liberals had not been defeated, but that the Tories had been elected. Having seen more than one Liberal government interred, I know how appealing it can be to attribute the cause more to one's cleverness than to one's luck. But I also know that while governments are often re-elected because of the lack of an alternative, they are invariably defeated regardless of one.

But you can understand the temptations. If you were Robert de Cotret or James Gillies, you would have wanted to believe you unseated a government as much for the wisdom of your economic policy as for the previous dearth of it; or if you were Bill Neville, because of the successful application of your game plan; or if you were Joe Clark, you would have liked to believe that you, too, had some hand in it. Taken together, congratulations were in order all round.

In such an insular mush of sentiment, notions of infallibility flourish. Since you had been so right, the chances were you always would be. When the clerk of the Privy Council, Michael Pitfield, flew out to Jasper to advise the conquering heroes on the rudiments of changing governments, so dazzled were the members of the new court of conquerers by the lights of their eminence that none could see his way to the airport to meet him. Pitfield, a doomed man, might have done better if he had arrived with a white flag. When he allowed — having been asked what he thought of a two-tiered cabinet — that he saw much against it, his opinion, of course, only clinched the matter. The upper tier of the two-tier cabinet, in its original composition, had no member in it from Toronto, or from British Columbia, or from New Brunswick.

It must have something to do with mountain air, a sense of euphoria induced by lack of oxygen. There certainly is evidence, from both the post-election and the pre-Parliament meetings, that while the scenic wonders of Alberta remain forever exemplary environments for rest and recuperation, they are deadly for the consideration of serious business.

I write this, I confess, not from clippings or from the record, but out of selective memory. Still, it seemed to me, as the new government inched its way towards grasping the levers and nettles of power, that it would have been smarter to have done its prep in Ottawa than in Lotus Land, even allowing for the fact that it was the prime minister's own turf.

The trouble with being out there in the seductive ambience of so much scenery and sycophancy is that one so easily believes only what one wants to believe. "Jasper was a disaster," a ranking Tory confessed to me. For out of Jasper (which was the pre-Parliament conclave of the upper-tier of cabinet) came the stubborn resolve that the Tories would stick to their guns — which meant that they were stuck with their platform to assist the home mortgage-holders and to remodel Petro Canada in the image of free enterprise.

Back in June, the cabinet had been sworn in, amid much public platitudinous regret as to its lack of Quebec timber. Still the *other* elected member from Quebec, Heward Grafftey, was given a portfolio that defied definition as to responsibility, while another member of the lower tier, Robert Howie, from New Brunswick, was slipped in as a glorified executive assistant to the Minister of Transport. What was missing was anyone with the experience of a George Hees, for one, or an Eldon Woolliams, for another. The Tories, used to eating their young, had now devoured their old.

Even so, it was a more promising cabinet than the one it replaced: David Crombie, Flora MacDonald, David MacDonald, John Crosbie, Elmer Mackay, Don Mazankowski, John Fraser, Ray Hnatyshyn, Ron Atkey — who could not be impressed, watching them take the oath and kiss the Book?

But against that cameo appearance of the many young lions at Government House at the swearing-in there followed the prime minister's news conference with its clangorous note of — well — of a peculiarly petulant defiance. The Tory platform, Joe Clark told the world, was no longer a matter for discussion, but a matter for action. On, then, to Jerusalem!

By then, I think, most of the damage had been done. By then, it became clear, public judgment of the new government was no longer suspended. There would be no honeymoon, not even a handshake, and no outpouring of voter goodwill showed itself in the polls. Instead, even before the Throne Speech, the government began a forced march

103

in retreat of its election promises — about which there was to be no further argument.

That hastily improvised plank in the Tory platform, the promise to move the Canadian embassy from Tel Aviv to Jerusalem, became a hangman's trap, providing the drop for Clark's credibility. The new, young prime minister never quite recovered from Jerusalem, that glaring exposure of his innocence, a demonstrated naïveté, which was, it has to be said, made more deadly for the bald political opportunism that was its motivation. Jerusalem hurt, not only because it exposed a weakness, but because it strengthened his enemies.

Further, while Liberals bury their mistakes — in the Senate or beneath a mount of righteous rhetoric — Tories manage to provide them with an eternal life of their own. Witness Jerusalem: rather than saying, as he is now saying, that the embassy move was a mistake — who is not entitled to err? — Clark finessed the issue with an inordinate cleverness. To disengage from a palpable blunder, he sent Robert Stanfield halfway around the world and back. Sure enough Stanfield returned to confirm the mistake in Joe Clark's campaign promise. Fair enough? No. Clark rerouted Stanfield around the world again, causing Stanfield to become a man in perpetual motion, who served to remind people not only that Joe Clark made a blunder in the campaign of 1979, but how difficult it had become to undo it.

The perambulation of Stanfield — even though undertaken with much dignity and minimal fanfare — *convinced* Canadians of the seriousness of the mistaken policy, even many who had thought little about it and were cheerfully willing to forget it. Far better, one would think, for Clark to have removed the policy early on, and abruptly let it be forgotten. (Indeed, it was, and remains, so delicate a domestic political matter that few Liberals have had the nerve to exploit the folly of it; but Clark has done that for them by keeping it alive, by putting Stanfield in perpetual motion as a sort of sandwich-man, bearing a sign that reads "We goofed!")

Jerusalem might have been a useful lesson in humility; instead, it became an inspiration to defiance. If the advisors were wrong about Jerusalem — and they were not admitting it, but merely manipulating the issue — they would hang tough on PetroCan and on the mortgage deductibility scheme: they would unite in a determined effort to salvage the platform that had come to represent their personal legitimacy in the seat of power. More than anything else, they had to assert not only the wisdom of their platform, but their authority. At the inner cabinet gathering at Jasper, the advice was "No more flip-flops."

Rocky Mountain fever!

The question of PetroCan, in the larger context of energy policy, was symbolic: it was, if nothing else, the only aspect of the energy issue that the public *thought* it understood — except only the issue of price. But PetroCan, as a symbol, grew in importance first of all because the case against "privatization" was so enormously appealing to commonsense, and secondly because the case for it was profoundly contradictory to the traditions of Canadian Conservatism. This contradiction explains why — even at Jasper — the Red Tories, such as Flora MacDonald and David MacDonald, and — yes — John Crosbie, were eager to leave PetroCan in place, while Clark's principal advisors were determined to muscle it into a position that would honour the platform commitment.

And what is the Conservative tradition? I submit that in two of the greatest challenges to nation-building — transportation and communications — the Conservative response was to create a federal agency or instrument, the Canadian National being one and the Canadian Broadcasting Corporation being another. If you like, add to that the establishment by the Conservatives of the central bank. In this most recent example of a national requirement — that of a secured energy supply — it was therefore heretical to the traditions of Canadian Conservatism to abolish the only federal agency with the competence to allow the government of Canada to take an active, interventionist role in national energy policy.

None of this mattered in the spring campaign: most Canadians were hot to defeat Trudeau, and merely bemused by the sight of long lines of motorists queuing at the pumps in the United States. Besides, Clark was promising energy self-sufficiency in a decade's time, not too long to wait for a people who were also told that, if anything, their expectations of the future were not rosy enough. The energy crisis, like unemployment, was something happening to someone else.

But later, in the face of the threat, more felt than understood, of substantially increased energy costs for home heat and the family car, PetroCan re-emerged as a symbol of ineptitude. For the average Canadian, feeling an anticipatory shudder, it made as much sense to sell off shares of PetroCan as it would to peddle the Canadian Armoured Corps to Hertz on the eve of a foreign invasion. Nor was it sensible, to the ripe wits and dour philosophers in a thousand morning coffee klatches, to give away half the shares of the corporation to Canadians, who believed they already own all of it. No, the policy advisors, struggling to save their pride, fashioned out of this whole issue the worst of achievement — a bad joke.

In August, when the provincial premiers gathered at Montebello, Bill Davis, the premier of Ontario, to the astonishment of many, abruptly staked out his case for holding the line on energy costs. Incredibly, the federal Tories concluded only that Davis, himself leading a minority government at Queen's Park, had committed a tactical blunder that would, in the end, only hurt *him*!

The rationale went something like this: domestic oil prices had to rise to something closer to OPEC prices (this in the name of simple equity for the oil-producing provinces); further, the public was prepared for and were willing to pay more now, in the interest of equity — and of conservation — and as a price for eventual self-sufficiency. Davis, then, was grandstanding, and — we'd all see — when the deal was made with Alberta, and the coming federal budget gave the promise of fiscal responsibility at long last, Canadians, Ontarians among them, would wonder why all the fuss. In short, while Davis was playing politics, the feds were practising statesmanship. And in the end, having taken the plunge to hold back on the rate of oil price increases, Davis — not Clark — would have painted himself in a corner. He might, in fact, even be defeated in a provincial election.

But let us examine some features of this strange and aloof attitude, this looking-down-the-nose from Ottawa at the man who had, in many minds, done more to give Clark his opportunity than any other politician, save only Trudeau himself. Clark had, after all, won his plurality in Davis's Ontario. In a province with ninety-five seats in Parliament, the Tories had taken fifty-six, and most of those in Ontario's industrial heartland.

One would therefore expect the Clark government, in shaping its energy policy, to take note of Ontario, the source of such a large part of its mandate. Instead they set their heart on a policy of self-determination, and ultimately self-destruction. The problem as they saw it was how to finesse past Ontario an oil-pricing policy that would satisfy Alberta. Given that Alberta's position on pricing was, rudely put, the higher the better, and Ontario's was the cheaper the better, the designated victim was certain to be Davis. One would have thought that the principal component in that consideration would have been the opposite: what is the optimum price that Ontario would pay to Alberta? But no, it was the other way around.

In this inversion of political strategy, the government was relying on a set of assumptions that proved to be serious miscalculations:

- that the federal government had time on its side
- that so long as Trudeau remained leader, the minority government was safe (and even safer once Trudeau announced his plans to retire)
- that Davis would have a provincial election to face in Ontario before there was a federal election
- that, all the above being true, Davis therefore needed Clark more than Clark needed Davis, and that once the energy policy pill had been swallowed by Ontario, the feds would then see

what they could do to repair the injured relations with their provincial cousins
- that there was, above all, *time*.

Well, all the above turned out to be wrong. More important, Ontario did the finessing: Davis showed his hand early, even while the federal policy was somewhere between gestation, resolution and negotiation.

Looked at from Queen's Park, there were three motivating reasons for the seeming haste to air Ontario's position. The first of these, of course, was that the federal policy was simply wrong, that it was not only bad economics but deadly politics. Reason enough, you might say, but there was yet more.

The second and third reasons involve some of the Davis personnel — such as Hugh Segal and Les Horswill in the policy and priorities secretariat, both of whom had served with Robert Stanfield in Ottawa, circa 1972-74. They knew, from that experience, the perils to Ontario of Clark's unfolding policy but, more, the perils to any party of having none at all. You could ask Bob Stanfield. At year end 1973, the minority Trudeau government stood lower in the public opinion poll than any Canadian government had in Gallup's history (until Clark's) — nineteen points behind the Conservatives. It was in the winter of 1973 when energy first emerged as a critical issue. During that winter and the early spring, while the Grits developed a policy response, the Tory caucus remained deadlocked between the opposing views of its western members and its Ontario members. When the government fell, or allowed itself to fall, Stanfield felt his party's failure to achieve a coherent energy policy had already lost the election. He still does; so does Segal. The issue of wage and price controls did not lose the election; the Tories had already lost it.

And, finally, the people around Davis had little use for the people around Clark. It was not that their relations were not cordial, friendly, even frank — but that those at Queen's Park had no confidence in the political judgment of their opposite numbers in Ottawa. What was hardest to bear, in the debate over energy policy between Ottawa and Queen's Park, was the realization that the feds weren't *listening*!

So the provincial Tories took a poll. Even better, they hired Allan Gregg, the federal Tory party's in-house pollster, to conduct the poll. Gregg's survey examined three questions: the state of Clark's popularity in Ontario at the time; the make-up of Clark's Ontario vote in the federal election; and finally, the sensitivity of the energy issue in the province.

The findings confirmed what most of Davis's advisors profoundly believed. First, that the federal government — and Clark — were already in trouble with the Ontario voters; second, that Clark's vote in the federal election had come largely from the hard core of Davis supporters; and finally, that energy — the cost of it — was now the major concern of the electorate.

The provincial Tories, who paid for the poll, asked only that Gregg furnish the relevant data to his Ottawa client, which he did. It failed to impress.

Horswill was even dispatched to Ottawa to brief the Ontario members of the Tory federal caucus on Ontario's position and warn them of the likely consequences of the proposed federal policy. He was given a rough ride. Curiously, the principal reason for supporting the federal policy was ideological. The time had come, Horswill was told, to get the government out of the energy marketplace, to allow the free enterprise system to work out the price, supply and demand for oil. Ontario, someone said to Horswill, was only being "parochial" — the rest of the country would support Clark.

And so it seemed at the subsequent first ministers' conference at which Davis, speaking for Ontario, was visibly isolated in his stand. There was, afterwards, a good deal of clucking sympathy expressed for Davis by the Clark people. As it turned out, they might better have saved it for themselves.

What followed, with the defeat of the budget in the House, was the fall of a government which was never to have the opportunity to demonstrate its worth. In summary, it was a tragedy of miscalculation.

By failing to call Parliament sooner than it did, the government insulated itself in a political vacuum of its own making. Since it heard no opposition, it saw none.

By assuming that it could not be defeated, it was prepared to run enormous political risks. The miscalculation was not so much one of arrogance as of innocence. It failed to comprehend the swiftness with which cynicism, opportunism and an abiding lust for power could combine to revive a defeated Liberal Party and even resurrect its leadership.

Somewhere, in the cosmos, Machiavelli and Mackenzie King are shaking hands.

10 January 1980

Elections serve to tell us — that is, the electors — as much about ourselves as they do about our parties and the political system. You could even say that, even while we are all in the process of making judgmental decisions about the politicians, the parties and their positions on public issues, we are at the same time making decisions about our own values and our perception of ourselves as citizens.

We are now engaged in an election campaign that is surely one of the most cynical, manipulative and wantonly irresponsible in our history. It is, furthermore, a campaign that is an astonishing affront to our democratic traditions, and one in which the fourth estate — our journalistic institutions — is a hapless accomplice.

For here we have a situation in which the Liberal Party appears to have an agreed-upon strategy by which its leader, P.E. Trudeau, the prime minister of Canada for eleven years, and who may yet be again, will not submit himself to questions from the media. And we have a party, now seemingly on the verge of an astonishing victory, which appears to have a policy, or a platform, about which they are prepared to tell us little or nothing. So that there is a clear conspiracy in the Liberal Party not only to conceal its leaders, to the fullest possible practical extent, but to hide its purpose as well.

I think all of this is inimical to the interests of a democratic society; indeed, is in defiance of those interests. It is something of a curiosity to realize that such a posture would be impossible to maintain in any other civilized nation in the world which has a tradition of democracy. And I am struck by the fact that the media, especially the newspapers, are so docile and accommodating in the face of it. Since we know the media is not powerless, then it can only be that much of it is gutless.

We have to ask ourselves — putting the question simply — why it is that Senator Keith Davey, the Liberal campaign manager, will not allow P.E. Trudeau, the Liberal leader, to be interviewed by the media? Is it that the leader is so ignorant of politics, or so compulsively candid, or so pitifully weak of argument that he must be hidden from public view? Or is it only that Senator Davey is convinced that his leader remains so despised and mistrusted a public man that he must be kept hidden from the electorate lest they rediscover their antipathy towards him?

There are no laws against this desperate cleverness which is at the heart of the Liberal campaign. But it is the long-established custom, a part of the tradition of our politics, that politicians are *public* figures and that the voters have the right, since they cannot do it themselves, to examine them on the issues and to have the opportunity to assess the substance of their case, which they do by giving their proxy to the media. The first politician we know of who sought to hide himself from the media in a campaign was, of course, Richard Nixon. But Nixon hid because of his paranoia, his own and that of his advisors, which told them the media hated him and were out to get him.

It is somehow grotesque that one of the most articulate and intelligent politicians in Canada, P.E. Trudeau, would run what is presumably his last campaign as though he were a frightened Richard Nixon.

There could only be two reasons for this: one of them the possibility that Trudeau has too much to answer for and dares not face the media; the other, that he truly has nothing to say, as to policy and program, that will stand up to public scrutiny. In other words, we are being asked to support a leader and a party whose position is indefensible.

On the other hand, the prime minister, Joe Clark, as vulnerable a public man as any could be these days, remains, nonetheless, accessible and available — and respectful of the democratic process. So that while there may be many duck jokes about Clark, how about a few chicken jokes about Trudeau?

But it is not, really, a joking matter. Or if it is, the real duck joke is on the Canadian electorate. For here we are, in the midst of much serious business which relates to the nation's agenda and to its future, and are we so childish, feckless and irresponsible that we will go on supporting this organized conspiracy of silence, which degrades our political institutions and insults our history? If we allow this to happen, if we honour the strategy by voting for its perpetrators, then we will have learned a good deal about ourselves, which is that we are unworthy of the responsibility of citizenship in a free society.

April 1980

It was a curious election, and as great as is my personal interest and absorption in Canadian politics, this one left me cold.

The Tory government of Joe Clark fell under the weight of its own crushing naïveté. It could not believe it could be defeated in Parliament, given the condition of the Liberal Party in the aftermath of its defeat last year. It could not believe it could lose an election, given the impressive rejection of the Liberal leader, P.E. Trudeau, less than a year ago. And it believed the electorate would respond affirmatively to a bromidic budget, promising "a short-term pain for a long-term gain." Is there a prize for naïveté?

We are all visceral utilitarians, and little wonder a sufficient plurality of the electorate voted Liberal, and for the Liberal promise of, well, a short-term gain for a long-term pain, if you like. You would have to be naïve yourself to believe anything else.

Of course, we are talking mainly about Ontario and, peripherally, about the Atlantic Provinces. Obviously, we are not talking about Quebec, where the voters, it seems clear, voted their history and their familiar bias, and not only against the budget but in support of the nation's least flexible federalist, the once and future prime minister of Canada.

110

There should be some consolation in all that. Given not only the body count of defeated candidates from the other parties — nothing unusual there — but as well the emphatic size of the majorities, the awesome scale and dimension of the rout, one wonders if Quebec has not now returned to a *status quo ante* Lévesque. English Canada, which had been nervously preparing some adequate response to Claude Ryan's option to separatism, will now cheerfully defer to Trudeau, whose constituency in Quebec is measurably greater than that of Ryan and Lévesque combined.

Nor is the mandate of the prime minister much diminished by the failure of the Liberal Party, once again, to win seats west of Winnipeg. Western Canada has long nursed the suspicion that, given time, the issue of separatism would go away, which may not be true; but at least the country is once more led by the one man who is least likely to concede too much in the struggle against it. One Canada has won again, and no prime minister could ever have been said to have such a free hand in grappling with an issue no one else, beyond Quebec, is anxious to seize.

Otherwise, appearances may be deceiving: the shifts and changes which brought about a Liberal majority were slight, and grudging. While Tory majorities dropped just about everywhere, most of them held. Where they didn't, the Liberal margins were in the main narrow ones. It was, remarkably, a joyless and reluctant electorate.

If Joe Clark was a liability going into the campaign, he became less so at the end of it. The Gallup poll, which showed the Tories trailing the Grits nationwide by twenty points since November 1979, may not have been wrong. It is at least as sensible to believe that Clark's dogged, determined campaign reduced the Liberal lead by half during the campaign. It is important, in the post-election celebrations and recriminations, to understand that the Liberal victory, other than in Quebec, was neither a rout nor a landslide, but a near-run thing.

None of that is worrisome to the winners or of comfort to the losers. The Conservatives have the burdensome task of reassessing their leadership, while the Liberals must, sooner or later, get around to choosing a new leader who will become prime minister. As well, the Tories will be poking among the ruins to find out what went wrong, while the Grits will be more pleasurably engaged in finding out what to do next.

Some Tories, of course, have already offered testimony at the inquest. The party's president, Robert Coates, the MP for Cumberland-Colchester North, has offered the view that the election result only goes to show that the Conservatives are not yet conservative enough and need to shift still further to the right.

As seldom as I agree with Coates, I have seldom disagreed more. But then, I have only said there would be a Tory post mortem. I did not predict it would be a sensible one.

The Maritimes Revisited

21 February 1979

Expatriate Maritimers who return home to live are nothing new. There are only more of them these days. They come back to retire, to weather their midlife crises, or to live out the fantasies they acquired after years sniffing auto exhaust in big city traffic.

Acquisitive, attuned, upwardly mobile Maritimers who have stayed at home to find careers are less likely to retire here, but take themselves to Florida condominiums, even as far as to villas in Praia de Luz, Portugal. This suggests they may have remembered something returning Maritimers had forgotten, such as Maritime winters, provincial tax levels, and the cost of bread. Show me a Maritimer who retires in the Maritimes and I'll show you a man who thinks he's smarter than K.C. Irving of Hamilton, Bermuda.

As for those who come back for reasons other than retirement, these must be clinical, or otherwise suspect. If it's not male menopause, it's something else as deadly. The answer as to how you're going to keep 'em down on the farm — now that they've seen Kitchener — has long since become, "Why bother?" Out-migration never did trouble true Maritimers, only their politicians. Besides, as they say, it reduces the competition. In-migration is the same, only in reverse. Expatriates who return, if return they must, to inflate property values and smile a lot, are merely something else to be endured.

Walter Gordon, who will be remembered in the Maritimes even after he has been forgotten elsewhere, once observed, through a Royal Commission in his name, that while Maritimers could never expect to

113

have it quite so good as Canadians elsewhere, there were compensations. These were listed as (1) the close proximity of fishing holes, duck blinds, and curling rinks, and (2) the historic, hard-earned right not to work overly much. Gordon's observations outraged Maritimers, and rightly so. They did not wish that kind of information given out.

The leaks notwithstanding, Maritime lifestyle remains our guilty little secret. Despite the unprincipled high cost of lettuce in February (largely due to the unrelieved factor of discriminatory freight rates, which forever bear heavily upon the region), it remains true that 47.3 percent of all Maritimers in managerial positions go home for lunch.

As an expatriate repatriated, and by no means the only one in these parts, I am in the happy process of rediscovering the Maritime lifestyle. The pleasures and delights are numerous, but they are not limitless, and adjusting to ways of doing things here, as compared to there (Toronto), requires patience, which in turn needs stoicism to sustain it.

Statistics Canada unemployment figures to the contrary, there is an awesome shortage of electricians, plumbers, masons, carpenters, surveyors, and people to cut hay. And it is seldom enough to find one or more of these to go on a job; you will often need to find others to finish it, since the Maritime lifestyle is, by nature, full of distractions: deer, moose, ducks, birds, racehorses and funerals, any one of which can summarily postpone, delay, interrupt or even terminate work in progress.

I see nothing wrong in this, although, as I said, it takes getting used to; put otherwise, it has been my experience that the more work there is to be done, the more enthusiastically and resolutely people will go at it. When there is little to do — such as finishing something — reluctance settles over the job, a characteristic I can only put down to being a genetic trait. (I now suspect Stonehenge was started by Maritimers — possibly it was to be an indoor Wiltshire shopping plaza — but they never got the roof on because of the opening of the werewolf season.)

At any rate, I am now living in reasonable comfort in my new, unfinished home here in Queen's County and I have a new, improved understanding of what is going on at Point Lepreau, where they have been, and will be for some time yet, building a nuclear power station.

September 1979

I would like to believe — as would most politicians — that voluntary conservation is a possible solution to the energy problem. But I don't.

Most of us grew up thinking the proper thing to do with energy was to consume it. So by now, instructing the children of conspicuous consumption on the adult virtues of energy conservation is like teaching cannibals to pickle beets: nothing in the history of their experience has prepared them for it.

Failing conservation, there is always rationing, which won't work either, though it would do wonders for the depressed post-war black-market industry. The third variable option in the conservation strategy is to raise the price of energy so high as to enforce the discipline of user-restraint. I know of no one driving around in a government car who does not believe that would work. Again, I disagree.

This vast country, we're so often told, was built upon the vision, courage and sweat of our forebears; but it now runs on gas, oil and the telephone. We are the world's most omnivorous users of each. When your average Canadian is not in his car, he's on the telephone, listening to his radio, or watching television. The truth about the Canadian automobile — like the instruments of Mother Bell — is that the car is not a convenience but a psychic necessity, and if governments push up the price of gas to compel Canadians to give up their profligate use of their automobiles, people will still buy gas and give up something else, like their children.

That being clear, we are now down to the ultimate solution, which is — are you ready? — to put an embargo on political sweet-talk about conservation and give earnest priority to developing alternate energy sources. What we are doing now is dithering over options we don't have, holding off the day when we will be obliged to confront those we do.

The most immediate, cleanest, cheapest option is nuclear power. I admit that when both Jane Fonda and Angus MacLean came out against nuclear power, it gave me pause. They have not always been wrong. But I am truly puzzled by Premier MacLean's position, which is, I take it, that when nuclear power becomes available from New Brunswick at a competitive price, he will nonetheless have none of it on Prince Edward Island. New Brunswick, which is a principal supplier to the Island, may deliver power it creates by hydro, coal, oil or sunflower seeds — but not by a Candu reactor.

Well, supposing — I have asked myself — that the New Brunswick Electric Power Commission, in the act of supplying its client with electricity, might one dark night slip a little nuclear juice into the grid and smuggle it onto the Island. Who would ever know? I mean, would there be a telltale blinking of lights, the smell of sulphur, or an ominous rumble in your humidifier?

Some of us tend to think of nuclear power as if it were one of the many options in technology down the road, such as solar heat or — a

115

contemporary Island favourite — wind power. But nuclear power is here, now, and whether one mourns or welcomes the fact, everyone will have to come to terms with it and, like it or not, become a consumer of it.

But we all need more information. One of my problems in developing a perspective on the energy crisis is that I don't know anyone who knows what I feel I need to know. For example, what do Premier John Buchanan and Baron Edmund de Rothschild say to each other when they meet to talk about harnessing the Fundy tides? Somehow, I tend to put the harnessing of the Fundy tides on that page of the Atlantic Agenda comprised of things everyone is in favour of, but no one gets around to doing — such as digging the Chignecto Canal or building the Causeway to PEI. The Fundy project, I realize, dwarfs all undertakings ever contemplated in these parts — something of the magnitude of bringing Newfoundland up to grade and paving it.

So when the Baron drops in upon the premier of Nova Scotia — a modern-day de Lesseps come to see the Sultan — I would like to be a fly on the wall, or at least an executive assistant, just to hear the conversation. Probably they get Bob Coates on the telephone first, before getting down to — well, that's it — getting down to what?

Buchanan's energy policy is as innovative as political realities will allow. He will import NB power for a short-term solution, employ Nova Scotia coal for a mid-term solution, and harness the Fundy tides for his grandchildren. The Baron, who believes we merely need $3 billion — or is it $30? — to get his show on the road, will only say he believes we are singularly blessed to have the tides to harness. A tidal bore of editorials surges in the wake of his departure, but no one really knows what it's all about.

If a food crisis erupted in this part of the world, there would be politicians who would favour developing the marzipan cookie as a remedial measure, providing only the necessary feasibility studies were undertaken.

You see what I mean. The energy crisis is real and will likely be felt by each of us. But not to worry: commonsense should tell us that, apart from whatever confusion may reign, we have always muddled through. You have only to watch the spawning of this new generation of ministerial, inter-governmental, international conferences, confabs, symposiums, and seminars on the crisis — enough energy expended to light the lamps of China — in order to believe it. So, keep the faith, and turn out the lights behind you.

As I read elsewhere in this magazine a few months ago, there has been a worrying increase in juvenile crime — mostly vandalism — on Prince Edward Island. Of all places, you might say. A Charlottetown alderman, searching for possible solutions, was quoted as saying, "Maybe a punch in the mouth will teach those kids some respect for authority." Well now. But do you think a kick in the ass would teach an alderman some respect for those kids?

I am something of an expert on the subject of juveniles because I used to be one and, as I remember, it was for a considerable number of years. Vandalism was not my cachet; I excelled at driving streetcar motormen mad by pulling their trollies off the wires. Given any reasonable amount of bad luck, I could have had a record myself and any number of missing teeth.

None of us, in our gang, came from underprivileged homes. Far from it, and much worse, we came from God-fearing, churchgoing families. To end this autobiographical detail, my personal career in petty crime and misdemeanors ended at Acadia University on a mild day in spring, when half the residents of Willett Hall gathered outside to smash out the windows of the old residence by hitting fly balls off baseball bats against the walls. Meanwhile, inside, the other half of the residents were lighting a fire, using broken furniture for kindling. I suppose you would call that white-collar vandalism, with a touch of arson.

Now that I am fully grown and about as adult as I'll ever get, butter no longer melts in my mouth. When I attend an evening social function and have a few drinks, I walk home afterwards — along with all the other law-abiding citizens who know the law and dread the breathalyzer. How else do we account for the staggering numbers of footsore pedestrians wending homewards from the Legions and the country clubs on a Friday night?

I don't even litter. But if you've ever been out on one of these spring-cleaning drives along our highways, the evidence is overwhelming that there must be hundreds of juveniles around who collect garbage in green bags and throw it out of speeding automobiles while their hair is growing and our backs are turned.

I do not presume to know what to do about the problem of juvenile delinquency. It's a problem we are, perforce, obliged to leave with social workers, the police, the magistrates, and — for laughs — the city fathers. Like aldermen. It does seem to me, however, that every society gets the younger generation it deserves, and likely no society has been so deserving of its juveniles as is this one.

117

The present younger generation has three things going for it, or against it, that my generation didn't have: television, pornography and drugs. Given the easy availability of each of these inspirational cultural activities, I suspect my personal history as a miscreant would have been considerably more impressive. Today's youth also has fast food, faster films, louder music, and the opportunity to pass through the entire public educational system without learning how to read. My generation was raised on a mother's cooking, the Hays Code, Guy Lombardo, and books with hard covers.

It does not take a miracle, these days, to produce any number of young folk who, as they approach their seniority, are already functionally illiterate, tone-deaf, ethically blind, emotionally retarded, and addicted to ketchup and fried potatoes.

The people who are pumping violence through the television tubes and into our homes are not juveniles. And they proclaim an adult's taste in entertainment, as the ratings indicate. The generation now roaming the shopping malls and hanging out under the street lamps was the first to be raised by the one-eyed babysitters produced by RCA and Hitachi. Why would they not reflect the behaviour their elders glorify for fun and profit?

As for the porn: the liberal-minded, such as many of us, still have some writhing to do with our modern, transistorized social consciences. On this issue, put me down as ambivalent. I merely think it a fitting and ironic commentary on our life and times that if you wanted to know what a self-proclaimed born-again Christian like Jimmy Carter had to say about lust, you had to go out and get yourself a copy of *Playboy* magazine. How do you think that strikes a young fellow who has been raised to honour his mother and respect his girl?

As I said, you won't find any answers here to the problems of Charlottetown and elsewhere. And while I don't much admire many of the members of the younger generation today, I don't envy them either. They have much to overcome and a lot to live down — most of which they got from the older generation.

Yankee Doodles

15 and 16 October 1968

Hubert Humphrey's "politics of joy" is contagious. The press, following his jet in two of their own, riding in his motorcade in laid-on buses, eating and drinking at irregular but frequent occasions along the way, are cheerful, relaxed and good-humoured. The politics of joy has not, as yet, infected the electorate, but the press have caught it.

As the 727 United jet rises from Washington's International Airport, and the wheels lock in the fuselage, the press applaud and cheer appreciatively. A voice on the intercom says: "Sock it to me?" Louder cheers.

The aircraft cabin is decorated with Humphrey-Muskie stickers, red and blue balloons, and hostesses who cheerfully ply the aisles distributing an infinite variety of food and drink, while Humphrey aides, all of them seemingly too young to vote, hand out revised itineraries, the day's prepared texts and miscellany concerning the vice-president's campaign.

Pennsylvania's twenty-nine electoral college votes are both vital and uncertain. Philadelphia is reportedly for Nixon, ten percent of everyone is for George Wallace, but on this day the vice-president will take soundings in the northern, lakeshore town of Erie and in Anthracite America — Wilkes-Barre and Scranton.

The flight of three jets land (another round of applause from the passengers), the Humphrey jet in the van, and the day begins. The first stop, described by one knowledgable reporter as "Dreary Erie," is a nondescript, two-storey, red-brick, small American city with a history of being helpful to Democratic presidential candidates.

The campaign obsequies for the world's most powerful office, and its most burdensome, does not differ much from those for the lesser portfolios in the outlying democracies. At the airport, some two hundred of the faithful are gathered, at the prodding of their local leaders, clutching homemade signs (the newest vogue) and accompanied by the inevitable high school band.

Hubert Horatio Humphrey steps from his jet, with its vice-presidential seal emblazoned on the door, his lightly tanned face locked in a taut, professional smile, and, as though programmed, works his way through a line of dignitaries, saying tonelessly and endlessly. "Hellohowareyou, nicetaseeya, thankyouverymuch." After that, he goes to the crowd, gathered behind a wire fence, shakes more hands, and then enters his car. The motorcade heads for downtown Erie. It could have been anyone, and it could have been anywhere in the free world.

The press follows in a fleet of buses, labelled "V.I.P.," "NATIONAL PRESS," and "LOCAL PRESS." There is none for FOREIGN PRESS, so I ride with the National, reading in the local press that HHH COMES TO ERIE, that the secret service has forbidden publication of the motorcade route, and that Senator Edward Kennedy has sent a telegram of praise to the vice-president for "your excellent address to the nation," the latter being an advertisement, in which it is clear that Senator Kennedy has endorsed Hubert Humphrey, "who has offered the American people a proposal for ending the war in Vietnam."

Erie produces a crowd for the vice-president's outdoor address. The square is filled with some five thousand people, half of them grateful children who have been let out of school for the day, some of them boisterous Nixon supporters, and a few of them peace militants. In this confrontation, on a chill, bright autumn day, one senses the uniqueness, and the sadness, in the life and times of Hubert Humphrey, the Democratic Party, and the American electorate, the special sorrow of the present American circumstance.

There is the usual clutch of city fathers, congressional aspirants, county chairmen and platform luminaries. To all this ageless ritual — they are introduced like prize-fighters at ringside, waving to the crowd and grinning — are added representatives of beautiful people and the American Negro.

For the beautiful people, there is Shelley Winters, who speaks with that half-remembered voice that is somewhere between a shriek and a groan, about something Eleanor Roosevelt once said to her, of her fondness for John F. Kennedy, of her mistrust of Richard Nixon and her dismay over the fact that he is leading in California. Miss

120

Winters says it is good to be back in Erie once more — "the last time I was here I was supporting John F. Kennedy."

Then Bobby Scott, "CBS recording star and author of 'A Taste of Honey'," is introduced. He says, briefly — mercifully — that he is going to vote for Hubert Humphrey.

Now they are ready to hear the man. One watches him and his audience, and, as he speaks, is aware of the struggle between them, the search for common ground and understanding, between one man trying desperately to reach the impossible summit of power on this planet, appealing to these few thousand of his millions of judges, who do not understand it, and whose comprehension of America's crisis of leadership is coarsened and clouded by frustration and violence and an inarticulate despair.

He has not the mien and manner of presidents; there is in him too much of everyman, with the pinched, narrow eyes, jutting chin, small, circular mouth, the slicked-down hair. History has found him among the dead, and he remembers what everyone for some reason has forgotten: that he has always been on the side of the little man, that his legislative record and his voting record are a monument to American liberalism. And that he is for peace.

In the struggle to reach them, there is earnest pleading. He says he spent the morning with Edward Kennedy. He quotes John F. Kennedy, in what must be one of his, or Sorenson's, lesser lines: "Republican policies have done nothing for you but they have done a great deal to you." He explains the special limitations of his office, and describes himself as "an advisor" to the Johnson administration. A minute later, he says his choice of Edmund Muskie as his running mate is "my greatest contribution to our country."

Someone in the crowd shouts, "Peace now!"

It was as though the vice-president had been waiting for it. He turns, thrusts out an arm and raises his voice: "You elect me your president and I'll bring this war to an end."

The crowd roars approvingly. Wonderful. The trade union placards wave, the hand-lettered posters wave; the heckling subsides. Later in the day, in Wilkes-Barre, the vice-president puts it another way, explaining how the quest for peace will be his first task, his constant interest, and that he believes he will succeed. Later still, in a university gymnasium in Scranton, he gives the short-hand version, again responding to a heckler: "You elect me your president and I'll bring this war to an end." The cheers are deafening.

What does he mean?

What one comes to like about the vice-president of the United States is his awful fallibility, his feet of clay, his transparent anxiety to flee his shadow, which is Lyndon Johnson, yet to remain what he has always been, a convivial, congenial, tolerant, loyal, regular fellow. What other major politician of our age could begin his speech by saying, "Mr. Mayor, my good friend Congressman Dan Flood, stars of stage, screen and television, ladies and gentlemen —" and mean every word of it?

In Scranton, before an audience of college students, he begins to digress by asking them rhetorically: "Did you watch the Republican Convention at Miami?" An electric shock went through the audience and someone shouted "Chicago"; whatever the point was to the question was lost as Hubert Humphrey scrambled back to his text. At an airport, he puts his arm around a young girl and tells her: "You tell your friends — don't opt out. Stay in. Tell them a Humphrey administration is gonna make the White House a mecca for young people."

We follow him to a tv studio for one of two local interview shows, each of them distinguished for their blandness and for the vice-president's encyclopaedic answers.

Outside the studio, a group of six youthful demonstrators stands by, placards at the alert. One of them is a teacher ("I also work for VISTA"), another wears a McCarthy button, and they are nervous, a little awed by their participation, and perhaps a little lonely. Shelley Winters goes to speak to them, but since they represent a generation of participants and not spectators, they do not know who she is. One of them thinks she is Susan Sonnberg and says so.

Miss Winters tells them of her acquaintance with Eleanor Roosevelt, and with John Kennedy, and that the only chance of stopping the war is Hubert Humphrey. One youngster holds a sign reading "27,000 dead, 166,000 wounded," over which a plastic skull has been fixed. He says, "That's what you said in 1964. You told us Barry Goldwater was bad, and so we got Lyndon Johnson."

"I can't disagree with you," says Miss Winters bleakly. "But I don't know anything about Johnson. I do know Hubert Humphrey. Being vice-president is a very difficult position."

A youngster says, as the rambling, inconclusive discussion ends, "Well, thank you for talking to us." As she leaves, they exchange knowing smiles. Never trust anyone over thirty. When the vice-president leaves in his motorcade, the police herd the young people back from the curb until they are standing under the trees, their signs hidden in the branches.

One of the newsmen quotes a remark he heard from the vice-president on leaving Scranton: "This is a helluva way to make a living."

And so it must seem to Hubert Humphrey when he thinks on it, if he does think on it. He can remember when the South was solidly Democratic. He can remember when friendly despots bossed the big cities — the likes of Prendergast, Curley, Hague, Crump and

Daley. He can recall when it meant something to have the endorsement of trade union leaders, when they spoke for their members.

Hubert Humphrey has not changed. Everything else has, while he retains the essential flavour and goodness of his age, that quintessence of American liberalism.

Encapsuled in a United 727 and homeward bound, a man reflectively stirs his martini with a ballpoint pen. "If Humphrey wins this election," he says, "it will be a disaster for the Democratic Party. If Nixon wins, it will be a disaster for the country."

4 October 1976

Portland, Maine — The ballroom, papered in a bordello red, was decorated with campaign posters. This is the year of the open throat in the Democratic Party: Jimmy Carter, Fritz Mondale, the vice-presidential candidate, and a local congressional candidate were all pictured on the walls, uniformly smiling and tieless. There was a free bar, and, at an adjacent table, a large wedge of local cheddar and crackers.

We were standing at the bar — where else? — talking to a young man who was measuring the crowd at this fifty-dollar per person Maine Democratic Party reception, at which the special guest is to be Jimmy Carter, the you-know-what for president of the United States. A secret service agent stood alongside, pretending not to listen, while the young man told us that he was really a Muskie man — Maine senator Edmund Muskie, that is — and that he was soft on Carter, so soft that he would probably vote for Eugene McCarthy for president.

It was a slim crowd, less than two hundred, and the young man said that it was more interesting to him who wasn't there than who was. Who was there, he said, were mostly lobbyists and who wasn't were the ranking Democrats, some of whom, like Muskie, were in Washington, others who might be at the airport meeting Carter's plane, and still others who were just staying away. While he spoke, a man behind us was badmouthing Carter for his *Playboy* interview. The critic was later identified as a lobbyist for the bottle industry, which is at present engaged in trying to defeat a referendum to restore bottle deposits in Maine. Whoever was there, it was not conspicuously a Carter crowd.

The candidate was late, as candidates usually are, and just before he arrived, a man made an announcement, asking the crowd "to spread out a little because this is a big room." Outside, there were twenty-five or so elderly ladies who had been seated in the lobby waiting to catch a glimpse of their man; someone sensibly gathered them up and let them into the room, as a sort of ballast, so that by the time Carter made his entrance, the crowd was not so noticeably thin, especially when someone else wisely turned off the lights of the three overhead chandeliers, plunging the room into semi-darkness.

My first impression of Jimmy Carter was that he is small. As he entered the ballroom of the Eastland Motor Hotel, surrounded by a phalanx of secret service agents, he looked like a coxswain out on the town with his crew. Up close, the face is lined and wrinkled, seared by a thousand Georgia suns. And, on examination, the Carter smile is indeed a physiological event; so prominent are the teeth, and so full are they in the mouth, that whenever the candidate parts his lips, the teeth, of necessity, emerge. Oftentimes, then, the expression is not one of radiant cheer, as in a smile, but the result of a necessary accommodation between too many teeth in too small a mouth.

On this occasion, the candidate wears a suit and tie. The tie is mute conservative and the suit is Sears Mail Order Gothic, a non-descript gray with a rust vertical stripe. He is introduced as "the next president of the United States," which causes neither protest nor conspicuous enthusiasm, and he steps to the microphone on the dais, lit by the glare of television lights, staring into outer darkness beyond, escalates the smile to the point of fission, holding it, like a man holding his breath, until the applause subsides.

The speech is brief and perfunctory, reflecting the painfully acquired caution of the frontrunner, which now discourages the impulse of either humour or candour. He has been to Maine five times, he says, and he has yet another speech to make at a downtown rally later this same night and — by the way — the money raised at this affair will go to the party locally and not to him, because "my campaign expenses are being paid by donations from the American taxpayers." For fifty bucks, it's not much of a speech, but no one expected more; the candidate makes his way from the room, pressing flesh, being embraced, and explaining he could not sign autographs "because the secret service won't let me."

Downtown, at the rally in Monument Square, Carter spoke for no more than twenty minutes, delivering a stock campaign speech containing much of the material used in the first television debate. But the crowd seemed to take it well and, when it was over, everyone appeared cheerful, including the several Republicans who had come bearing Ford/Dole placards.

As to the numbers attending, I estimated the crowd at two thousand; a secret service man said he thought it was "between four and six thousand"; the *Bangor Daily News* reporter called it between seven and ten thousand; and the *Boston Herald* estimated ten to fourteen thousand.

And that's about it, from Portland, Jimmy Carter-wise. Driving back from the rally, it suddenly struck me that Carter reminds me of Wendall Wilkie, the populist Republican who ran against Franklin D. Roosevelt in 1944 and whose principal asset was that no one knew anything about him. They still don't. But Wilkie lost, as you so well remember.

25 April 1980

The Canadian response to America's abortive attempt to free its hostages in Iran has been sympathetic and muted. The Soviets, naturally, are holding their sides in mirth. But whether clucking or laughing, as an initial reaction, second thoughts may be improved on sober reflection.

What sticks in the mind, and craw, is the abiding suspicion that Jimmy Carter's high-risk enterprise was the product of a mind too preoccupied with domestic considerations involving his own political skin. Otherwise, it makes no sense.

The military operation must have assumed casualties, including the deaths of at least some of those who were to be rescued. It could have been, had it gone further, a total disaster. As it is, the mission qualifies not only as an operational fiasco but a calamity for the president and deeply disturbing to America's friends.

I have a hard time justifying in reason the trade-off Carter was prepared to make. What we know of the condition of the hostages indicates they are alive and reasonably well. Beyond that, world opinion has been coming increasingly to America's side. While her friends have been encouraging patience and restraint, many were also responding to requests that they themselves give tangible evidence of their support through sanctions and other measures.

Furthermore, should any of the hostages be harmed by their captors, world opinion would not stand in the way of punitive American retaliation against Iran. But Carter has short-circuited this gathering of world opinion and compromised the moral strength of his position by this feeble, futile resort to armed force, which, even had it been carried through, would have been a bloody, savage business at best. It must seem to some who have been and remain sympathetic to America's dilemma that Jimmy Carter has become more anxious to punish the Iranians, as solace to his nation's pride, than to secure the safe release of all the hostages.

And now, having cast away so much credibility and having squandered more national pride on the Iranian desert than was in ransom, Carter has blown away his chief claim to the presidency — that, unlike Governor Reagan or Senator Kennedy, he was a prudent, cool and safe man in a crunch. This misadventure, after all, raises at least as many doubts about Carter's judgment in a crisis as have been raised about Kennedy's, after Chappaquiddick, or about Reagan, whose rhetoric sometimes seems to suggest that he might be trigger-happy.

As a result, Carter is also a casualty, and I suspect the recrimination over his folly will be closely followed by retribution at the polls. At the very least, he has liberated Senator Kennedy, if no one else. The Democratic convention in New York City may be a significant political event after all.

Thus, in assessing the damage, we shall find that Carter's presidency has been seriously weakened and his campaign for re-election critically damaged, while the Iranian government has been immensely strengthened, and America's friends must find their support wavering in the face of such awesome incompetence.

The episode is, as well, a further reminder of the limits of power, even of a super-power. But that Jimmy Carter had to find that out for himself, given the illuminating examples bequeathed him by his predecessors, is perhaps not so remarkable as it seems.

Not until the primaries and the election are over can we afford to take another deep breath. Meanwhile, I'm wearing a Mondale button.

2 July 1980

Perhaps you've noticed an increasing amount of twitchiness among Canadians as it becomes increasingly clear that the next president of the United States might just be Ronald Reagan. Since the era of Franklin Delano Roosevelt, if not because of him, the vicarious participation of Canadians in American presidential politics has grown. As many Americans did, we revered Roosevelt, respected Dwight Eisenhower, and liked John F. Kennedy. Given the chance, they all could have carried Canada.

But the perception of Reagan in this country is clouded by apprehension and foreboding: as a politician, he is pretty well everything Canadians prefer not to see in an American president. He appears to be an ideologue, whereas we lean heavily to pragmatists; he is a neophyte in foreign affairs, an almost certain disqualification even for our own potential leaders; Reagan is also a Republican, an old one at that, and Eisenhower was the last, and only, Republican president who was genuinely popular in Canada; finally, Reagan comes from California, which is not a border state but a territory known to produce bumper crops of political eccentrics, of whom Governor Jerry Brown is only among the latest.

By Canadian standards and tastes, Reagan is not a world-class politician. Of course, by the same measurement, neither is Jimmy Carter, a further reality which imposes upon us a somewhat novel dilemma: which of these two presidential candidates do we least want to win?

Canadians are familiar with such harrowing considerations in their own electoral processes. But since most of us have been, historically, closet Democrats, it seems likely that, come November, Carter will get from us a grudging nod. Still, it's a long time from here to November and, speaking for myself, I'm not sure I won't end up casting an absentee ballot for Reagan.

The fact that the apparent Republican presidential nominee knows very little about world politics — or, as Clare Booth Luce once described it, "globaloney" — may be less a liability in a world in which no one else appears to know much either. The first time John Kennedy sat down with Nikita Khrushchev, the Russian had him for breakfast; when they collided some time later in the missile crisis, Kennedy's acquired reputation as an uncertain innocent abroad made him dangerous enough to cause the Soviets to back off.

Carter has been a notorious overachiever and a moralist in the bargain. The trouble with that sort of posture is that one has the appearance of waving a big stick while in a prone position. But Reagan's morality, mercifully, is confined to domestic causes; he is not out to save the world from perdition but merely to rescue the American family. No one ought to object to that.

And certainly Reagan's rhetoric on overseas issues has been known to be bellicose on occasions: if words had been deeds, he would have blown the Panamanians out of the tub before yielding the canal and he would have paved Vietnam to make it a parking lot.

As to the latter, Reagan might have had a better idea — in view of current events — than those who thought it would be nice if the Americans sent money and care packages to assuage their guilt. But my point is that if one must choose a president based upon his promise of performance in the foreign policy field, one is tempted to foresake a president whose approach has become recognizable for its indecision and excess flab, in favour of one who appears to have no pretensions of reforming the world and who will not be so much indecisive as he will be unpredictable.

It is not true to say of the western alliance, of which we are a charter member, that it is only as strong as its weakest link. It is, instead, true that it is only as strong as its strongest link. America's present weakness, which becomes our own as well, rises out of a confusion of defence priorities and a sense of purpose blunted by diversions, distractions and dubious enterprise. And I don't believe Jimmy Carter can ever get it all back together again.

Perhaps Reagan could. He may be, in his time, something of a throwback to another Republican of sorts — Theodore Roosevelt. They all laughed at Teddy for his patriotism and for what seemed to some a simplistic view of America in the world. But it worked for America, and until and unless something else does, American foreign policy won't work either.

17 August 1980

The party of all the people except the very rich came out of New York's Madison Square Garden reasonably intact, sort of united, and with some hope yet of beating the Republicans in November. Family farmers, however, should not bet next year's crop on it.

The Democratic convention was great theatre; had the show opened on Broadway, it would have had a long run. The final act on Thursday night was not climactic, but it was not without high drama and low comedy. As with all politics, the process often becomes pure pageantry: the totemic figures of "Tip" O'Neill, Coretta King, and Martin Luther King Senior; the ritual observances of magnanimous winners and gracious losers; bands playing from the party hymnals, "Happy Days Are Here Again" being to a Democrat what "Onward Christian Soldiers" must be to a Baptist; and, of course, the cast of thousands on the convention floor, miming their roles as celebrants, soreheads, and assorted political wheels for the unseen onlookers in videoland.

The rites of winners and rules for losers were, alas, only partly observed by Jimmy Carter and Teddy Kennedy. The senior senator from Massachusetts came reluctantly to the platform for the closing ceremony, bearing one of history's most chilling smiles; when he left the platform soon after, it was deep in permafrost. The Kennedy-Carter vignette offers further example of a familiar reality in politics: nothing is more dangerous to the prospect of success than too much planning for it too early.

Even before Carter was to make his acceptance speech to the convention, containing his effusive tribute to Kennedy — an extended olive branch large enough to put the entire Kennedy delegation under its shade — mortal damage had already been done to the prospect of a successful reunion by planners on the Democratic national committee.

128

Before Carter spoke, and with Kennedy surely watching the proceedings from his hotel room, the committee presented its film, packaged weeks or months ago and before anyone, much less a film-maker, could know the climate and condition of the convention at its conclusion. There must have been an assumption, however, that by the time this pretty paean of praise for the president would be viewed by the delegates, Kennedy would have been disposed of and left twisting in the wind. It did not turn out that way: by the time the film was shown, Kennedy had miraculously become the healthiest man in the Democratic Party.

At the top of the film, a voice well oiled by unguents of sanctimony set forth the necessary qualities out of which great presidents are made. The first of these, intoned the voice, is that the president of the United States must be "of strong moral character." What might appear as a truism to many, or even a banality, might also be heard as a rebuke to a man whose moral character had been held in serious question — had indeed become a matter of open discussion — from the moment he had declared his intention to contest the nomination against the incumbent president.

Kennedy had reason to feel, at long last, that he had faced the issue of his character and had overcome it; at the very least, as a man preparing himself for a sporting assignation with the Democratic ticket, neither he nor his followers needed reminding of the superior moral character of Jimmy Carter, as perceived by the Democratic national committee.

And, really, did anyone else? And, anyway, how pertinent is the truism? That strong moral character might be the first quality for a man who would be president requires elaboration or explanation. It is, after all, also a necessary quality for banktellers, journalists, and even members of the United States Congress. But those who are truly possessed of it do not need to advertise it, unless to remind others of the risk of hiring or electing someone else who just might be short of it.

It looked to me, watching Kennedy en route from hotel to convention platform, that he was not so much resigned to appearing on the platform with Carter as he was outraged by the requirement to do so. For all the vulnerability and sensitivity of convention losers, accepting defeat is one thing, but taking insults is another. Thanks to the master-minds who manage Jimmy Carter, an argument could now be made that stupidity may be more deadly to a politician than even a flaw in his character.

The Fudge Factory

While I was out of town it came to pass that everyone's favourite hardware salesman — Lockheed Aircraft Corp. of the USA — employed the services of a newly established consultant's firm, Reisman and Grandy Ltd. of Ottawa, Canada, whose two principals had recently retired from senior posts in federal government service.

According to impeccable sources, namely Messrs. Simon Reisman and James Grandy, the consultants were not employed to contact the government in Lockheed's interests, or vice-versa, but, as Mr. Grandy explained, his firm was employed to "advise Lockheed on such things as the difference between the operations of the United States govern-ment and the Canadian government."

A man who purports to be a retired RCMP stable-hand has passed on to me a tape-recorded telephone conversation which he found in the flap of his underwear when he changed it this spring. I don't exactly know what it really is, but it plays like this:

Operator: Good afternoon, Reisman and Grandy Limited.

First Voice: This is Lockheed Aircraft calling. I want to speak to either Mr. Reisman or Mr. Grandy.

Operator: Just one moment, Mr. Aircraft, I'll connect you.

2nd Voice: Hello?

1st Voice: Hello. Is this either Mr. Reisman or Mr. Grandy?

2nd Voice: Yes, it is.

1st Voice: Well, we here at Lockheed have been reading a lot about your Olympics up there, you know?

130

2nd Voice: Yes, in Montreal, Quebec.

1st Voice: Right. Well, we here at Lockheed have been reading about your Olympics and we thought your country is the sort of place where we here at Lockheed could do some business.

2nd Voice: The objects of our company are to carry on the business of management consultants, industrial consultants, systems consultants and advisers and consultants in the operation of all kinds of business. . .

1st Voice: Well, look, what Lockheed really wants to know is the difference between the operations of the United States government and the Canadian government.

2nd Voice: That's what you really want to know?

1st Voice: Right. Lockheed has had considerable experience around the world and we know how a lot of governments operate. But we can't find anyone who knows how your government operates.

2nd Voice: Sir, it's like we were made for each other. We mesh at the right interface, so to speak.

1st Voice: Right. So tell me how it operates up there in Canada.

2nd Voice: This is strictly confidential — but not all that well.

1st Voice: Like we always say at Lockheed, nobody's perfect.

2nd Voice: Canada has a parliamentary system of government, with a prime minister and a cabinet. The cabinet is appointed by the prime minister from among the elected members of Parliament.

1st Voice: How about that!

2nd Voice: There's more. The cabinet makes all the policy decisions and all cabinet ministers are collectively responsible for the policy decisions of each individual cabinet minister — it's called collective responsibility and cabinet solidarity.

1st Voice: We sure couldn't work that way here at Lockheed. I mean, you'd have chaos.

2nd Voice: We have that here, too. In our Canadian system, only the cabinet decides on policy. The civil servant, however wise, carries out government policy, but he or she doesn't make policy.

1st Voice: Well, what about generals, air marshals, and admirals? Who makes their policies?

2nd Voice: In the event of war, military policy is made by the prime minister alone. In peacetime, every effort is exerted to avoid having anyone make policy.

1st Voice: Look, suppose some guy wanted to sell a few airplanes up there? I mean, who do you talk to and how. . .

2nd Voice: I'm afraid we're drifting a wee bit from our terms of reference. Have I told you about the Senate?

1st Voice: My God, you have a Senate too?

2nd Voice: We have a bicameral system. Senators are not elected by the people but appointed by the prime minister. They are appointed for life, or until they reach the age of seventy-five, when they enjoy a pension. But Canadian senators do not make policy and have no power to change policy.

1st Voice: Jeez, that's incredible. I'm sure glad I called you.

2nd Voice: As we proceed, you will find many differences between the operations of this government and that of the United States — or Italy or Japan, for that matter.

1st Voice: I sure hope so.

2nd Voice: Well, before we get into the Canadian banking system. . .

1st Voice: I'd like to get into that as soon as we can.

2nd Voice: First, perhaps, we should discuss our fee arrangements and formalize our relationships, contractually.

1st Voice: Sure. Besides, I don't think I can absorb any more right now.

5 November 1976

When I first met Bernard Ostry, some twenty years ago, I was at my desk in Bracken House, that old ramshackle two-storey dwelling on Laurier Street, Ottawa, that served as the Progressive Conservative Party's national headquarters. He had come to talk to me about a book, *The Age of Mackenzie King*, which he had co-authored with Henry Ferns, whom I did not know and have never met.

I was impressed by Ostry's directness, clarity and incisiveness, and, above all, by his self-assurance. In the idiom of a later time, he was cool. In the climate of that day — the mid-50s in Canada — he seemed to me to be also brave, even brash.

After I read his book, a copy of which he had left with me, I was even more impressed. What young Ostry, then twenty-five, and his colleague, ten years older, had done was write a well-researched book on Mackenzie King's career, prior to his assumption of the leadership of the Liberal Party, that was — well — critical. It was, the authors confessed modestly in their preface, "presented to the reader not as a definitive study, but as an essay contributed to a public discussion of the thoughts and policies of [King]."

But even so modest an ambition proved to be pretentious. Though the book deserved "public discussion," it did not get it. Its first edition of some four thousand copies disappeared, presumably sold; there was no second printing. The rest was silence.

In its day, the book ought to have been something of a sensation, a publishing landmark. It stripped layers off the myth of Mackenzie King, exposing his deviousness, his notorious ambivalence, his ruthless cunning, and plain dishonesty — all of which helps to explain his unique success as Canada's supreme politician.

And yet, such a book does King, the politician, no disservice; it only does justice to the truths about him and, if you like, about the age of his ascent to power. He was, indeed, a man who could encourage striking workers to stay out while encouraging their employers to stand firm, and while condoning the hiring of goons — all at the same time. He could sympathize with the wretched lot of the open-strip coal miners in Colorado, and, at the same time, sympathize with their neo-despot employer, John D. Rockefeller Jr. And also take his money.

Given an audience of Germans and their descendants, he could criticize Robert Borden's naval policy, which was, as King put it to them in 1911, to help Britain "to build warships to fight Germany." Such was not meant as prophecy, but as self-serving demagoguery.

There was, I think, a conspiracy to keep the truth about Mackenzie King from the Canadian people; certainly, there was a conspiracy to create a myth about him. The fact that we now appear to know so much about King — even, one might say, more than we ever wanted to know — is due more to King himself than to his biographers. Ironically, King withheld nothing; it's all in his assiduously kept diaries. The official biographers were in on the cover-up.

The trouble with the Ferns-Ostry book, written twenty years ago, sniffed the academics, was that it had been produced without access to the King papers, which were all at Laurier House, being laundered, sanitized and expurgated so that biographers would be neither diverted nor titillated in the canonization process.

The Laurier House biographers and researchers were much like a wartime spy ring; each of them might know something, but none of them would know everything; the place was not so much the prime resource for King scholars and biographers as it was a fudge factory.

In such an atmosphere, young Bernard Ostry came to Ottawa from New York, on a scholarly mission. It was, simply, to pursue his book on King by assaying the material in the national archives, such as the public papers of Sir Wilfrid Laurier or Charles Murphy. He spent a couple of days sorting through stuff, establishing himself at a desk, busily accumulating reference material he thought relevant to his work. On a subsequent day, he returned to his desk to find it bare. Everything had been removed. Not only removed, but, as of that moment; hidden.

When Ostry inquired of the staff as to this strange occurrence, he was told any papers he had found, and might yet find, were now "not available." When he appealed to the Dominion Archivist himself, Dr. Kaye Lamb, he was told, "You can't have them."

Now, the Dominion Archives is a public place — like a park — and the material in it is public property. But the archives had been suddenly closed to Ostry, without apology or explanation.

He sought advice. Someone suggested he speak to Leonard Brockington, who was, among a number of things, a kind of orator laureate, a friend and admirer of the late Mackenzie King and purportedly an executor of the King estate. Ostry found his man in the law offices of Duncan MacTavish, a Liberal senator and fund-raiser. For some reason — and having known the gentle, kindly man slightly, I suspect it was his innocence — Brockington agreed with Ostry: even a man writing an unauthorized book on Mackenzie King had his rights in the Dominion Archives.

The advice given Ostry was interesting. First, don't air the matter on "The Hill" — meaning among opposition politicians; second, see Jack Pickersgill, who was the clerk of the Privy Council and also a custodian at Laurier House. Brockington arranged, by telephone, for Pickersgill to see "this young man."

Ostry went to the East Block, found Pickersgill, and told him of his interest in Mackenzie King. Pickersgill then proceeded to enlighten him; Ostry had, after all, come to the Official Source. Finally, Ostry managed to ventilate his problem with the Dominion Archivist. Could Pickersgill help?

No, Pickersgill told him, he could not.

"But all those papers are in the public domain," Ostry protested.

Pickersgill remained adamant. It was then that Ostry asked him what right the clerk of the Privy Council had to deny anyone access to the public archives.

"Would you please leave," Pickersgill said.

It would have seemed to someone less determined that the public archives were closed to him. Not Ostry. There was, then, a war of attrition, the scholar insisting upon his rights and the establishment resting on its authority. Finally, Ostry won; he returned one day to his desk to find the documents had been restored. As suddenly and mysteriously as the doors had been closed to him, they were now reopened.

Well, not entirely. It is a lesser point, but it is a point nonetheless that, from then on, Ostry discovered entire volumes of Laurier's papers — essential to a study of King's early career — had been removed from the Archives and sequestered in Laurier House, ostensibly for King's biographers. While this was not the day of the Xerox, it was well past the time of the invention of microfilm. What

134

had been transported to Laurier House, which was considerable, was original material, yet no facsimile had been left behind.

There are two possibilities. The demands of King's biographers — over at the fudge factory — were so voracious that they had been given, through some fiat, first priority over all the material in the public archives. Not just priority, as Ostry learned, but exclusive use. Or, another possibility: someone, somehow, wanted to prevent anything being published about Mackenzie King, at least until the official authorized version had come from Laurier House.

In 1955, Ferns and Ostry produced their book. If it had been difficult getting at some of the source material in the Dominion Archives, it was impossible getting recognition for the end product.

While visiting Ottawa, Ostry once noted, in the CBC's program listings, that *The Age of Mackenzie King* was to be reviewed on the national network. And by none other than Fred Gibson, who was working with MacGregor Dawson, King's first official biographer, over at the fudge factory. It was doubtful the review would be favourable, but, nevertheless, it would be aired to a national audience.

Alas. Something happened along the road from the fudge factory to the CBC studios; the program was cancelled. Gibson had written the review, all right — he told Ostry that — but the CBC had told him to forget it.

Ostry, who was, and perhaps still is, a hard man to put down, made inquiries of the CBC as to why the program had been killed. No one knew. Gibson didn't know, he had only written a book review. Bernard Trotter didn't know. Bob Weaver didn't know. E. Davidson Dunton, the president of the CBC, may have known — but would he tell? Tell Ostry? Donald Fleming raised the subject in Parliament; no one knew there either, of course.

So the book was submerged, smothered in silence, sunk nearly without trace. The *Journal*'s Grattan O'Leary reviewed it. The academic community sniffed around it; some suspected bias, a federal offence.

I guess you could call this a typical Canadian success story. After all these years, *The Age of Mackenzie King* has been republished, by James Lorimer & Co., book publishers to the anti-establishment, among other things. But critical appraisals of King have become almost fashionable. We have journeyed a long way, from MacGregor Dawson and Jack Pickersgill, the early biographers, to Professor C.P. Stacey, and the reminiscences of Bruce Hutchison. There is, so to speak, a lot of Mackenzie King hanging out, and few are left who still cling to the myth. Most are content with the man who has emerged; he is no longer the one-dimensional plastic Laurier House original.

Still, I find so much of the writing on King to be bloodless. God knows a lot of it was gutless. King still suffers from the fact that his biographers were all sprung from the same era of Canadian history, out of the same condition of the Canadian society, which were very much of King's making. One would gather, reading Stacey, that the old fellow might have been kinky, or reading Dawson, that he missed sainthood only in the recount, or, reading Pickersgill, that he was a major bore, or, reading Hutchison, a minor mystery.

Ferns and Ostry revealed him as the consummate politician, with an unquenchable thirst for power, and the implication left with us is that it takes that sort of aberrational being to govern this country for so long and as successfully as King did.

We are now free of the King mythology. The mythologists have been routed. Some of the credit for that goes to Professor John Saywell, who, it may be remembered, blew the whistle on the fudge factory. It was Saywell who first reported — out loud — that the King diaries were being bowdlerized by the overseers at Laurier House. The outburst may have broken an eleventh commandment — I think scholars allowed on the premises of the fudge factory were obliged to swear to something akin to the Privy Council Oath — but Saywell gave us the first hint of what was going on, and thus hastened the downfall of the myth-maker.

But it need not have taken so long, and, frankly, that is what interests me more than the books now being published, and more than King himself.

We were, in the 1950s, a curiously passive country and a remarkably submissive society. The travails of Bernard Ostry, doing his book on Mackenzie King, are as illuminating of the era King established in Canada as of the age that formed him. I have, for two decades now, admired Ostry for his stubbornness and tenacity, and wondered how he came by it.

The answer is that he was less shaped by King's Canada than most; he was more shaped by the London School of Economics, the postwar sentiments of the European Christian Democrats, and by a life in the United States. He was too young to have been either patronized, proselytized, or prostituted by King's Liberal Establishment.

For so many others, coming off the Great Depression, or World War II, or both, arbitrary power and authority were familiar and synonymous. One did not buck the establishment; there were two generations of Canadians who had become thoroughly experienced in tugging their forelocks before their bosses, or saluting their superior officers. For many Canadians, subservience was a lifetime career.

Mind you, I think the story of the Ostry-Ferns book is funny. It is authentic Canadian humour. Does anyone know of an aspiring author, anywhere in the free world, who was thrown out of his nation's public archives? By the chief archivist? Or, of a scholar going to a ranking civil servant, pleading to be allowed back in? Or, of being stonewalled by otherwise decent, talented people who cannot tell him why a review of his book has been cancelled by the national broadcast service? Could it happen in Britain — or New Zealand?

The most extraordinary thing about it all is that no one thought it extraordinary. Mackenzie King ruled Canada, and after him, his heirs and assigns — Louis St. Laurent, Pickersgill, the Liberal Party, and the upper echelons of the civil service. Of them all, it could be said King elected them, or appointed them. And he also empowered them.

In those dear, dead days of national tranquillity, our two solitudes, and the romantic notion of "the unknown country," the glory was God's and the power was Liberal. It was comfortable, even cosy, if conformity suited you. It suited most.

It was, more than anything else, a state of mind. We were governed by people who simply could do no wrong because they knew everything they did was for the right reason. In the aftermath of King's death, this epic piety, self-righteousness and arrogance lingered on, and as much as we were confined or tranquillized by it, in the end, they themselves were more cruelly deceived by it. While we were led to believe in their essential infallibility, the notion did no great harm until they believed in it themselves.

Looking back, I wonder if anything like it will ever again settle on the land and upon its people. Ostry and Ferns think not. Ostry is now a prominence in the federal public service. Ferns is a professor at a redbrick university in Britian, a social democrat become a Tory. He had once worked for Mackenzie King; he now knows Enoch Powell. Who knows if their judgment has improved as much as their station? A quarter of a century ago, they were more discerning, critical and diligent than most, if not all, of their peers.

I like to believe *The Age of Mackenzie King* was the brave beginnings of a critical analysis of political events and politicians in this country. It freed up expression, gave fun to the chase, and liberated Mackenzie King, the most important politician in our history, from his biographers. Were it not for Ostry and Ferns, and perhaps for the pipeline debate, and maybe the corruption of the Speaker — were it not for these — all our history might still be coming from the fudge factory, and all our scholars yet convinced that the world is flat. And Liberal.

It is well known by every student of Canadian political pathology that the central nervous system in the Canadian body politic is motivated by a pendulum powered by an eternal transistor. So that while turtle-neck sweaters, or zero-based budgeting, long hair, or regional desks will each have their vogue, you can bet on it that they will soon enough become unfashionable. You can, that is, if you can find someone silly enough to bet they won't.

The pendulum being where it is these days, which is to say as far right as it can swing, there is a brisk competition among our politicians as to who can be the least compassionate, the meanest, the most gimlet-eyed, and the most devout in protestations of faith in the dogma of free enterprise.

That it would be easier to pass through the eye of a needle than to enter the kingdom of Heaven without a balanced budget is the recently revised scripture of governments and opposition alike. Neckties are in; so, also, are nooses. It is somewhat novel still, to me at least, to learn that what's good for General Motors is indeed good for Canada.

It's not been all bad, of course. It is pleasing to see a Liberal government, at long last, retreating from the wasteful folly of universality in social benefits. And I am comforted by the seeming resolution to stop the endemic habits of bureaucratic empire-building. True conservatives, myself included, have been saying as much for years, and judged as heretics for it.

But I am troubled by the dull and spiritless mentality in all this frenzy of retrenchment and budgetary blood-letting, and by much of the rhetoric that accompanies it.

It strikes at credulity to have the federal government, seemingly at least, confirm the fact that it could reduce its expenditures by some two billion dollars. Not that it has, or not even that it will, but only that it now says it could.

It is of some interest to note how the government would go about it, if indeed it does go about it. It would dishonour its commitments to pay bilingual bonuses to its civil servants; it would shut down a fisheries research station in Halifax, which has been in operation for forty years; it would take an axe to the CBC and savage the already meagre appropriations for the Canadian arts; it would welsh on some $370 million previously promised the provinces. The ultimate result of the government's indiscriminate zeal could only produce a further harvest of frustration and despair, of which we already have a bumper crop.

What we can say, from the evidence, is that we have had a profligate government for too many years when we needed a prudent one, and that what we seem to have now, rather than a chastened government, is merely a blindly malevolent one.

As one who believes the CBC to be something of a national asset and who is confirmed in the view that public support of the Canadian arts is essential to their survival, I find the government's proposals appalling, but revealing.

The Philosopher Prince, as P.E. Trudeau once appeared to be, emerges now as something more like King Herod. The government, having drawn the sword against budget deficits, is off slaughtering the innocent.

In this relentless re-enforcement of the business ethic in government, which is the orthodoxy of reaction, we could yet achieve a balanced budget, but with a national communications system given over to the profit motive and commercialism, in a country from which many of our most gifted people have fled.

Profit being the nation's penultimate priority, we might see shares in the government of Canada, or in the National Liberal Federation Ltd., quoted on the New York Stock Exchange. And elected politicians, coming to their offices each day, would not make a move without first calling their brokers.

But of course not. This, too, shall pass; the pendulum will swing. Perhaps even so soon as the spring of 1979, when some brave soul may emerge from one or other of the political parties and appeal to our nobler instincts and aspirations. It is true, he or she will say, that we have been living beyond our means — but still, fellow Canadians, we must all have the means to live.

Conscience, charity and compassion will again flood the public soul, and we will be back to running governments at a loss so that the whole of society may enjoy the true profit of belonging.

16 July 1980

Politics, when you get down to it, is numbers. After you've sifted through all the value judgments and decisions made by those who are elected to make them, you'll discover that that which is right and good to do is that in which the numbers are right. And by numbers, I do not mean statistics or even the numbers on the currency to be spent, but the numbers of *votes* involved.

When the votes to be counted in the decision are few, the politicians take cover under lofty principle, homely virtue and shibboleth. No, they will say, we couldn't do that because of budget restrictions, or it's really not our business, or it's unconstitutional. Then there is also the business of free enterprise: in our society — ahem! — the state has no business in the boardrooms of the nation, which is vernacular for the established aphorism in conservative dogma that government which governs least governs best.

Walter Reuther, a dominant figure for a quarter of a century in the labour movement in North America, and in the United Auto Workers in particular, once remarked that he could see nothing wrong with free enterprise save he would be happier were it less free and more enterprising. Reuther, who was somewhere along the political spectrum between social democrat and Marxist, did not live to see the day, now upon us, when a number of governments, notably those of the United States, Canada and Ontario, had intruded themselves into the boardrooms of the automotive industry, not to regulate it but to bail it out.

The governments providing the lubricity of cold, hard cash to the industry are made up of Democrats, Liberals and Conservatives. The Chrysler Corporation has been granted a $1.5 billion guaranteed loan from the Carter administration (and a relative amount from the Canadian government), while the rest of the auto-makers have been promised immediate help in financing their inventories of unsaleable cars with further loans — the ball-park figure suggested being between $200 million and $400 million, presumably depending upon how many cars Detroit can't sell. But that's not all, nor enough, as President Carter has been quick to add.

But apart from ready cash, the auto-makers would like something done about the competition, of which there is plainly too much. It's been cold out there in the free marketplace, and the cries we hear coming from the jungle of capitalism are those of free enterprisers from Detroit who have been treed by meat-eating Volkswagons, Datsuns, Toyotas and Hondas. What Detroit (and Windsor) say they need to survive is more protection in the form of higher tariffs, import quotas, or tax incentives for motorists who drive domestic cars. Or all of those.

It can't be said any longer by the devout believers in the free market, free enterprise and the iron rule of the bottom line — profit or perish — that the trouble with politicians is that they have never had to meet a payroll. In the example of the automotive industry, we are looking at the ultimate entrepreneurs, who have been given their heads for years, bringing us the airflow sedan, planned obsolescence, genuine imitation naugahyde interiors, pectoral fins, wrap-around chrome, and clocks that didn't keep time. As Reuther was saying, they were a good deal freer than they were enterprising. Today, they're hanging around the showrooms, kicking the tires and waiting for their government cheques. If it's made in America, the next car you drive will have been on welfare even before it had wheels.

Contemplating this rush of solicitude from governments, accompanied by our money, which is being showered on a struggling industry, my mind goes back to the famous Bricklin car, put together in New Brunswick a few years back, but now a museum piece in Ottawa, standing alongside the McLaughlin-Buick, where it continues to be admired by children of all ages.

The Bricklin, you'll recall, floundered and failed from the cashflow syndrome — there wasn't enough of either — and help was denied it by dozens of agate-eyed bureaucrats, cold-hearted politicians, and other creditors. Ottawa invested a million, but closed out the account thereafter. But saving Bricklin was a piece of cake compared to salvaging the Chrysler Corporation.

Still, there are more federal seats in Ontario than in New Brunswick; more people in Windsor-Detroit on the street on Sunday morning than in all of New Brunswick anytime; more entrepreneurs in the boardroom of General Motors than on the Bricklin assembly line. The help you get from your government depends on the numbers.

If you're small and don't need much help, you get none; you get to help those who are big and need a lot. It's called free-enterprise socialism.

25 July 1980

When William Lyon Mackenzie King abolished the practice of Canadians being knighted, elevated to the peerage, or gonged with memberships in household orders of the British monarchy, a sizeable vacuum was thereby created in Canadian society. For some years after, Canadians who had earned some special distinction, or a lot of money, went without recognition by the state. Those who had achieved excellence were left to enjoy their loneliness, or a bad press. Perhaps King's largest contribution to Canada during his interminable stewardship as prime minister was to make egalitarianism the prime virtue of Canadian citizenship.

When a girl named Barbara Ann Scott became our first national heroine since Laura Secord, by winning the figure skating championship of the whole world, the best an adoring nation could confer upon her was the honour of having her picture taken with Mackenzie King — and a car. Later on, perhaps because cars were becoming more expensive, the government of Canada finally got around to establishing the Order of Canada, with various ranks and elevations, our very own gongs, which could be worn around the neck if you owned a tuxedo, or otherwise as a discreet boutonniere.

141

You can get the Order of Canada in various ways, all of them natural and familiar enough to anyone who has ever read an Honour's List on New Year's Day; which means you qualify if you have brought distinction and credit to yourself, thereby the country, by performing some duty, act, or service exceptionally well for a period of time or all at once. And to show you how far we have or haven't travelled from our colonial past and Dominion status, Canadians receive their awards from the Governor General, who is Her Majesty's senior satrap in the land, even though, to be scrupulously honest, Her Majesty has nothing whatever to do with the selection.

It was incumbent upon the founders of the Order that it be seen to be distinctly Canadian and — to be sure — that it be consumedly non-political. To ensure the latter, a select nominating committee was established. Among the screening committee's non-political present members are Gordon Robertson, a retired Ottawa brahmin, Michael Pitfield, a rehired one, and Pierre Juneau, once the Liberal candidate in Hochelaga, all of which might amuse you.

On Friday last, a special investiture was held at Rideau Hall, where His Excellency bestowed Orders of Canada upon the heroes of our embassy in Teheran who sheltered and liberated seven Americans who would otherwise now be hostages or dead. There will not be any dispute among Canadians that the ceremony was a fitting one, recognition being truly deserved.

Speaking as a mere untitled, egalitarian Canadian, I have to say, nonetheless, that this latest investiture was a disappointment, and I am not alone in that view. One of the most deserving and conspicuously heroic in the Teheran caper went unrewarded, which suggests that there ought to be a further committee established for inexplicable oversight.

What such a committee would have found was that Zena Sheardown, the wife of John Sheardown, the Canadian embassy's immigration officer, sheltered, fed and otherwise attended five of the seven fugitive Americans in her home throughout the long and hazardous period of their being in hiding. It should be clear to anyone who knows anything about the Iranian adventure, let along anything about keeping house, that Mrs. Sheardown's contribution was extraordinary and far beyond the call of mere hospitality.

Zena Sheardown is, however, not a Canadian; she was born in Guyana and travels under a British passport. Notwithstanding, there is provision in the articles of the Order of Canada for awarding honorary membership to non-Canadians. Messrs. Robertson, Pitfield, Juneau et al will be a long time finding a more deserving non-Canadian to recognize, although perhaps they are awaiting the second coming of Charles de Gaulle.

Anyway that's how the cookie crumbled among the senior diplomats in External Affairs, who did not nominate Mrs. Sheardown,* and maybe that's how the world presently turns. But you've heard the line about there being a great woman standing behind every great man. It takes nothing away from John Sheardown to say that, in the heroics of those who ran such high risks in Teheran, it could be said to have been the other way round.

26 December 1980

The other evening, I found myself in a television discussion on the subject of neo-conservatism, the flowering thereof and its likely harvest, as though any of us would know. My companions were Fiona Nelson, chairman of the Toronto school board, and Barry Callaghan, a professor on the York University faculty. However much our musings enlightened the viewer, they were at least illuminating to me.

To begin with, both Nelson, who has NDP bona fides, and Callaghan, who Will Rogers would have described as a "nothinarian," confessed to having interwoven in their personal ideologies positive conservative strains. Without their admission, I would never have guessed it, and while I would sooner be drawn and quartered than imply their admissions lacked conviction, it also suggested to me that conservatism has recently come out of the closet. It is now safe, even fashionable, for consenting adults to admit to their conservative impulses.

It needs saying that both my fellow panelists described themselves as qualified conservatives rather than neo-conservatives. Still, the Tory congregation is overflowing the temple, while lapsed liberals are leaving empty pews in what was only yesterday the largest political denomination in our part of the world. And whereas an elasticity of doctrine allowed almost everyone short of H.L. Hunt and Enoch Powell to qualify as liberals, similarly today's renascent conservatism includes a wide spectrum of believers, a gospel tent large enough to accommodate the disciples of Margaret Thatcher, Ronald Reagan, and, yes, Joe Clark, George Grant, Lubor J. Zink, even unto John Turner, who may become the first Blue Grit — the new flip-side of Red Tory — in Canadian politics.

What we have, as this political realignment gathers force, is not a clearer definition of conservatism, but a more acceptably confused one.

*A spokesperson for External Affairs swiftly assured me that the Department had nominated both Mrs. Sheardown and Mrs. Taylor. Some fifteen months later, justice was done.

Given the rising numbers of adherents and their successes elsewhere, if not yet in Canada, conservatives may now enjoy the same rights to pragmatism and ambiguity that liberals previously presumed were their exclusive entitlement. What will likely be left to the liberals is the nugatory posture of being merely anti-conservative. The wheel and the worm have both turned — it is now the liberals who must explain themselves.

The fall from favour of liberalism is not without a bill of particulars. Of the many public resentments against it, the two most popular are that liberal governments used inflation as a cowardly alternative to increased taxation for the purpose of bridging the growing gap between their incomes and their excesses; second, through their adventures in social policy, liberals made work a spectator sport. When the roof fell in, as it has in the US — the jurisdiction with the most influence upon Canadian political thought — what remained was a mountain of debt, the rubble of social policy, and an inviting prospect for a conservative renaissance.

But if liberalism has deserved its fate, the question is not yet answered as to whether conservatism will be deserving of its opportunity. Despite its newfound popularity, there are grounds for concern and caution. The move to the right has been, and will be, nudged along by an omnibus of interests, not all of them appealing, some of them not even democratic.

In the consortium of interests, it will depend on which rises to the top. But there is a clear and present danger of a growing autocracy and, in the name of conservatism, the entrenchment of special privilege and of private economic power without public responsibility. Dwight D. Eisenhower, who has been perhaps the most underrated of American presidents (soon to be re-evaluated), described himself for the record as a "militant liberal." It was a warning to those who saw their opportunity in Eisenhower's enormous mandate to redefine conservatism to suit their own interests. It might be timely for those politicians now riding the conservative crest to sound the same alarm, or conservatism's sudden fashion will last no longer than the mini-skirt.

Other Men's Flowers

The Globe & Mail, 4 December 1976

One *Canada, Memoirs of the Rt. Hon. John G. Diefenbaker.* Volume Two: *The Years of Achievement 1956-62* (Macmillan)

In the beginning, John George Diefenbaker counsels us: "Journalists may write their worm's-eye views. Prime Ministers deal with broader vistas."

I liked that good juxtaposition, a generality with gossamer glints, the put-down of an enemy caste, the exaltation of both office and office holder and, as with every sentence, paragraph and page of this second volume of the memories and memoirs of John Diefenbaker, unabashedly self-serving. And why not? What are memoirs for, if not vindication?

"If you only knew," he used to say to his crowds, "the burdens of this office." The private agony of decision, the misery of being the prisoner of secret truths, athwart those broad vistas, a man standing alone, and, worse, the only man who knew.

"If you only knew," he would say, hinting at a knowledge too complex, confidential or privileged for those who had to view life from way down there, where the worms are. We listened open-mouthed to this burdened man whose lips were sealed.

But hearing it — "If you only knew" — one worm could say to another, "If we only knew *what?*"

Well, sometimes there would be dark hints — if we only knew about a detractor in the press, or a defector in his party, or the president of the United States, or if we only knew about "they" — could it be choice gossip or classified material? — if we only knew the something that ranged from rumour to dossiers.

Then we would understand the burdens of that office, and we could understand George Hees, Leon Balcer, Flora MacDonald, John F. Kennedy, Lester Pearson, Oakley Dalgleish, Jim Macdonell, Earl Rowe, George Nowlan, George Hogan, Eddie Goodman, John Bassett, Donald Gordon, Crawford Gordon, Walter Gordon, Gordon Robertson, Robert Thompson, Doug Harkness, James Coyne, the Siftons, Southams, *Maclean's*, Tom Kent, Norman DePoe, Eaton's, the CBC, CFTO-TV, the *Globe and Mail*, the *Toronto Telegram*, the *Toronto Star*, the *Winnipeg Free Press*, Kathleen Kearns, George Drew, Bay Street, Wallace McCutcheon, Christopher Soames, Mitchell Sharp, Pierre Sevigny, E. Davie Fulton, John Foster Dulles, Allan Dulles, those "Pearsonalities" in External Affairs, the federal civil service, Joey Smallwood, Blair Fraser, Max Freedman, Bruce Hutchison, General Norstad, Richard A. Bell, Tom Bell, Mother Bell, "they" and "them" and "those who" — to name a few, that, if we only knew, that is, knew what he knew, we would then know.

Robert Kennedy once described the philosophy which governed his relations with the press: never complain, never explain; get even. Diefenbaker had his own; get even. This is pretty much the essence of Volume Two — getting even.

Of E. Davie Fulton, once a protégé and close confidant, Diefenbaker recalls that when he appointed Fulton to the Justice portfolio, he had reservations: "He was politically ambitious, and, as Prime Minister, I had always to consider this when reviewing his recommendations to Cabinet. Furthermore," he adds, by way of clinching things, "he was not politically wise: three of his great finds as officials and assistants in the Department of Justice were Guy Favreau, subsequently Minister of Justice under Pearson, Marc Lalonde, Minister of Health and Welfare under Trudeau, and Michael Pitfield, the present Clerk of the Privy Council."

Keep in mind, the words are from a man who deals "with broader vistas."

I mean, what sort of indictment is it of one man's judgment of other men's talents that he would have given employment to such a trio — two of whom would later become ministers of the Crown, and another who would become the ranking public servant in the land?

The poignancy in all this is that Lalonde and more likely Pitfield might have become active Conservatives — but neither could stomach Diefenbaker. I only know that from Lalonde; reason allows me to believe it of Pitfield.

146

As for the luckless Favreau, he was to be driven from office, broken by the Rivard *affaire* in which he was a mere accessory after the fact; a busted minister because his prime minister, Lester Pearson, suffered either a lapse of memory or a deaf ear. Anyway, Favreau is dead. Most who survived him speak well of him.

The important thing is that Diefenbaker thinks it's important to the jury — perhaps conclusive — this evidence that Davie Fulton hired Grits — GRITS! — while he was the Tory minister of justice. On the other hand, Diefenbaker's trusted friend, Howard Green, was appointed to Public Works so that, in the awarding of government contracts, "the integrity of the government would be unchallengeable."

It is interesting — this passage about cabinet selections — because it is abundantly clear that Diefenbaker did not see his colleagues as equals in any sense. There were some he trusted and some he didn't, some who were too ambitious to suit him, and some who had, in his mind, superior "personal integrity." Although many of them, in the end, did conspire against him, it seems fair to say that, from the beginning, he was conspiring against *them*.

The trouble with Leon Balcer, who had fought a good Second World War, who had come from Trois Rivières to the Tory caucus, and who learned to speak English by a daily reading of the *Montreal Gazette*, was this: "Although I found him honest," says Diefenbaker, "no uxorious control have I ever known to equal that in which he was enmeshed."

Almost anyone reading that masterful convolution will skip over it, satisfied that, while the precise meaning is far from clear, the sense of it has somehow been imparted. Balcer was honest — a relief, surely? — but he was an uxorioutor, actually enmeshed in uxoriousness, which, one suspects, is the kind of thing, if you were ever into it, you should take a cold shower for, or attend confession, or have some chicken soup. One could suspect that uxoriousness, if not checked, could do untold damage to one's uvula.

Like so much else in Volume Two, this is not easy for the worms to understand. Still, worms are not without imagination, and they could imagine how Diefenbaker, as prime minister, drove strong men to drink and their wives to despair. Wives of politicians are not without influence, because even a politician's wife has feelings. It is as true of Fran Harkness, or Pat Fulton, or Mabel Hees, or of Eva McCutcheon, as it is of Genevieve Balcer.

. . .When the wife of Pierre Sevigny told the wife of Leon Balcer, just before the Diefenbaker government collapsed in 1963, that her husband was quitting the cabinet, as was George Hees, and as should Leon Balcer, Genevieve Balcer said — in effect — the hell he is, and she fought openly and fiercely against it. So Balcer stuck, was re-elected, and went on to become Diefenbaker's designated George-Etienne Cartier — at least for a time — and even his chosen seatmate in opposition.

Diefenbaker can be unrelenting, writing of his enemies, including those he identifies and those he doesn't, and whether they are living or dead. But, given his nature, it is not so surprising. Perhaps more surprising, he can also be stinting in the recognition of some of his friends.

He pays glowing tribute to Gordon Churchill as a distinguished educator, parliamentarian, strategist, and "a strong man," though he does not explain how Churchill began as his minister of trade and commerce and ended up in veterans affairs. But one is surprised at the scant recognition accorded Alvin Hamilton, whose seminal mind initiated and influenced, we all believed, so much Conservative policy. Possibly there was something we didn't know about Alvin.

"I have never had a ghost writer to draft my speeches for me," Diefenbaker writes, and, later on, informs us, "A teleprompter turns speakers into amateur announcers."

Well, Don Johnson ghosted speeches for Diefenbaker, so did Roy Faibish, Merril Menzies, Grattan O'Leary, and so did I. All of us, at one time or another, have stood at the back of halls and heard our words over the heads of crowds, a host-to-ghost private hookup between those who packed the snowballs and the man who threw them. And Diefenbaker was good at it; certainly he gave "the stuff," as he called our offerings, the unique gift of his own delivery. He could pitch the slowest curve in the English language; he could throw junk balls, fast balls, sliders, and bean balls. In his prime, he had the best delivery in the trade, and the record to prove it.

As for Alistair Grosart, who managed the winning campaigns of 1957 and '58, Diefenbaker described a vital part of his role as that of "a conduit collecting my speech materials."

Let me tell you how that worked. The crucial speeches in those campaigns were the 13½-minute orations delivered over the national television network. They attracted the largest audiences, and demanded the most careful preparation. So, when one of these major speeches was due, and wherever Diefenbaker was on the campaign trail, Grosart would materialize, red-eyed and near exhaustion, but with the text in his hands, to be delivered to the originating station so it could be put on the teleprompter.

After that, Diefenbaker would arrive, formally greeted by the management and then taken to be made up for his performance. On such occasions, his radar would be in full operation, scanning the station manager, the producer, floor director, camera crew, and teleprompter operator for possible saboteurs — if we only know about some of *them* — and he would have a rehearsal and then he

148

would do it. Often enough, words would be changed, a sentence deleted, or a paragraph rearranged. But, in the end, he would deliver the speech almost as Alistair Grosart wrote it. Whatever else any of us thought of Alistair in those days and we thought a lot of him, we never quite thought of him as a conduit. I still can't.

This is an astonishing book from a man who promises us a view from the broader vistas, where prime ministers have reserved seats. Every Tory should read it, certainly, and the world's historians must read it, just in case they think they know it all.

"He [President John F. Kennedy] hated Britain, and did not conceal his attitude," writes Diefenbaker. See what I mean? There is some indication, based on early returns, that Kennedy disliked Fidel Castro, Charles de Gaulle, and John Diefenbaker, nor was Nikita Khrushchev a special favourite, but that he "hated Britain" is incredible news. It puts an entirely new light on Harold Macmillan, who apparently was too dumb to recognize it, and on Sir David Ormsby-Gore, who was very nearly a personal ambassador to Kennedy from the Court of St. James, and summons into conjecture all that any of us — at worm's-eye level — ever believed about American-British relations during the brief Kennedy presidency.

One of the most revealing sentences in Volume Two is this one, which is a part of the recounting of Diefenbaker's first meeting with President Kennedy in January of 1961:

"Nor did he [Kennedy] ever comment on the subject of women in my presence."

Nor did Charles de Gaulle, surely, nor Solomon Bandaranaike, Harold Macmillan, Pandit Nehru, nor Konrad Adenauer. Or did they? Perhaps in the decade the CBC has now established as Diefenbaker's Own, world statesmen spoke of little else. Could it be?

No. This remarkable statement — a grammarian might call it an inserted insinuation — that Kennedy did not talk to Diefenbaker about women, back in 1961, is just possibly meant to remind us, long after the president's death, that a woman companion of Mafia chieftains allowed as how she had slept with Kennedy. All of which goes to prove further that Diefenbaker was, all along, right about Kennedy. Camelot, you see, was a cat house; Kennedy had diversions, Diefenbaker had vision.

His speech to the United Nations in 1960 was a personal triumph (Grattan O'Leary helped write it), but later, recalling the event to a Canadian audience, Diefenbaker directly related his speech to the episode in which an enraged Nikita Khrushchev banged his shoe on his desk. Good stuff, except the worms down below said it wasn't so. Volume Two puts the matter in another, later perspective:

"The climax, however, did not come until some days later in the Assembly debate when Senator Sumulong of the Philippines, *in recapitulating my arguments.* . .It was here that Khrushchev totally destroyed his credibility by waving his clenched fist and taking off his shoe and slamming it on his desk."

One is reminded of what someone said of the British historian Macaulay: he wished he could be as certain of just one thing as Macaulay was certain of everything. Volume Two is not just Diefenbaker triumphant, but Diefenbaker transcendent. Still, I am saying it is a valuable book. Even though he has forgotten much he should have remembered, and remembers much more that should have been forgotten, Diefenbaker's memoirs are devastatingly telling because they tell us more about him than he intends.

There is something approaching magnificence in a man who is eternally at war with his enemies, including whole battalions of those once his friends, but who, unlike most of us down here at ground level, remains sublimely at peace with himself. It is his passion never to be wrong, his tenacity never to admit he could have been wrong, and his genius, when something clearly went wrong, always to put the blame squarely on someone else, all of which gives him his remarkably unique character.

But then, as he continues to remind us, "If you had only known." Indeed — if we had only known. But at least we're finding out.

The Globe & Mail, 5 November 1977

One Canada, Memoirs of the Rt. Hon. John G. Diefenbaker. Volume Three: *The Tumultuous Years 1962-1967* (Macmillan)

John F. Kennedy came from Camelot, where he ruled with maid Jacqueline, holding perpetual court among the eternally beautiful people, Harvard intellectuals, successful men of crisp assertion, seeming immortals in a world of wit, style, elegance, grace, wealth, yes, and power — awesome, ultimate, Armageddon-like, thermonuclear power.

When confronted by Camelot's might, Nikita Khrushchev blinked, Harold Macmillan was accommodating, Charles de Gaulle and Konrad Adenauer went along, but not John George Diefenbaker, the prime minister of Canada. He stood.

In Camelot, however, John Diefenbaker was only a five-letter word.

Diefenbaker's country was Byzantium, exquisitely complex, barren, subterranean, remote, buried in snow and impenetrable rhetoric. There were no streets in Byzantium, only mazes, no court, and many cabals. Outside, at the gates — enemies; they were rich and powerful, of course, but then, so too were the enemies *inside* the gates.

"The big people finished me — the most powerful interests," the Leader told a supporter in 1963, after the fall.

Inside the gates were nests of traitors, armies of assassins, marauding bands of journalists, Communist sympathizers (in high places), blackmailers, continentalists, *deux*-nationalists, mischievous judges, ingrates without number, and heavy drinkers.

Unlike Camelot, Byzantium was a hard country to govern; indeed, as it turned out, impossible. Still, as the Leader has written:

"It was said I had no guiding right to the Leadership. . . But those who took up this cry missed the point that I had not received my mandate from the party's great and powerful, but from the average Canadian. *I knew to whom I was accountable. . .*"

Ah, the Average Canadian! And who was that? Apart from the slight statistical data available — 69 years old, 2½ children, Protestant, wearing white socks, with a lifetime pass on the CNR — the Average Canadian, it was believed, faced North every morning, where the Vision was, looked South with apprehension, and on Quebec, never. The trouble was, after 1968, the Average Canadian failed to turn out in sufficient numbers for elections, or for Byzantium's annual meetings, or even for leadership conventions. So far as we know, the Average Canadian came to shirk his role of political activist; instead, he wrote letters to the Leader.

Average Canadian letters sustained the Leader of Byzantium. Whenever — which was often — the knaves, rogues, scoundrels, and the plain wrong-headed closed in upon him, the Leader went off to read his mail, from whence he would return to tell them all that the Average Canadian had just written to urge him to take a stand, which he did. He stood for the Red Ensign, the Royal Coat-of-Arms on mail trucks, for the Bomarcs but against the warheads, for bilingual cheques but against the Official Languages Act, for One Canada, and for the Average Canadian (from whom he received annually a renewed mandate by direct mail). Byzantium's Leader stood, and stood, and stood. And stood.

Let us now proceed by illustration, gleaned from pages of the Official History of Byzantium, written by the Leader himself:

"Malcolm Wallace McCutcheon. . .was Canadian business's Mr. Big, one of Canada's leading industrialists and financiers. . .He pretended to be my friend. . .

". . . I hoped McCutcheon would be my answer to Kennedy's McNamara. . .It does not take long to gain the measure of a Cabinet colleague's capabilities. . . Given his general lack of aptitude for things

151

governmental, I would never have imagined he seriously entertained political ambitions. Had anyone told me at the time. . . he was at the centre of meetings designed to develop and encourage dissent within the Cabinet, I would not have believed it. Of course, no one did tell me until it was too late; not a word, not a boo. It was, I suspect, McCutcheon's wealth that drew to him certain types of hangers-on, be they Cabinet Ministers or whatever, much in the way a magnet attracts paper clips."

McCutcheon — Diefenbaker's "error to end all errors" is described here in impeccable Byzanteese. The Leader would have no truck or trade with the rich and powerful, yet he sought out the richest and most powerful — "Mr. Big" — made him a Senator and Minister without Portfolio (Byzantium's answer to Camelot's McNamara) and while Diefenbaker says he soon recognized McCutcheon's lack of aptitude for "things governmental," he promoted him anyway, to be his Minister of Trade and Industry, even though McCutcheon was not only without aptitude but also without loyalty, except that no one told the Leader, but then he would not have believed it anyway, if someone had, although, looking back on it, McCutcheon drew people to him — "hangers-on" — because of his wealth, but, unlike the Leader, who was drawn to him, the others were more like paper clips, although these included Jim Johnson, the Leader's most trusted national director, who was originally a McCutcheon protégé, and Johnson's immediate predecessor, Dick Thrasher, who later became Diefenbaker's executive assistant and, after that, McCutcheon's chief organizer in his bid for the leadership, in 1967, when Diefenbaker was also a candidate. You see how simple it all is, in Byzantium?

If McCutcheon personified the Leader's ultimate error, the distinction was narrowly achieved:

"Alistair Grosart. . . indicated a desire to retire from his position as the Conservative Party's national Director. . . Unwittingly, I contributed to my own difficulties by the appointment of Dalton Camp as his successor. At the time, I was unaware that he was the anointed of the McCutcheon group."

Now, this is *high* Byzanteese; your average scholar would never unravel it, as deceptively simple as it appears on first reading, because, you see, Dalton Camp did not succeed Alistair Grosart as national director; Dalton Camp never was national director.

Nor was he just another paper clip. It is true that he was offered the position of national director, early in 1963, by Gordon Churchill and others, on behalf of the Leader, but he turned it down. (At that time, McCutcheon was trying unsuccessfully to anoint Mel Jack as national director; taking on the job of national director in

152

those days was like signing on as helmsman for the *Bismarck*.) However, Camp did serve as chairman of the National Campaign Committee for the purposes of the imminent 1963 general election, a position that was voluntary, unpaid, and, obviously, forgotten in the official annals of Byzantium.

As consolation, however, is the Leader's final judgment of that election campaign: "I declare that there was nothing in the 1963 campaign that, in the light of events then so regarded, I would now change."

Except the Butterworth letter. But in Byzantium, exceptions are always the rule; except, of course, where they are not.

J. Walton Butterworth was the US Ambassador to Canada. During the 1963 campaign, a letter alleged to have been written by him to opposition leader Lester Pearson fell into Diefenbaker's hands. It contained such pearls as, "It will be quite evident to the electorate that the policy of the Conservatives is narrow-minded and that they are unfit to continue governing the country."

The letter was so monumentally indiscreet — "I would like to discuss with you how we could be useful to you in the future. You can always count on our support" — that one had to conclude that either Butterworth was a dolt or the letter was a forgery. Diefenbaker has no doubts:

"I have since concluded on the basis of confidential knowledge, *which will be revealed in due course*, that it was a true copy, and that not using it constituted a major political error."

Now we know he knows it was a true copy — just how is a revelation yet to come — but if his confidential knowledge is as sound as his memory of how he got the copy of the letter, then we are all in trouble — you, me, Butterworth, and future historians.

The Diefenbaker version is that "I received a copy. . . postmarked Acton, England. . . two weeks before the election. I was campaigning in British Columbia at the time. . .There simply was not time before the election, given the rigors of the campaign and the fact that we did not know who had sent us the copy, to determine whether it was a forgery."

Well, we did know "who sent us the copy." It came from George Drew, then the Canadian high commissioner in London, innocently carried, in a sealed envelope, across the ocean by J. Alphonse Ouimet, president of the CBC, who turned it over, at Dorval Airport, to Roy Faibish, then on the Tory election campaign staff, who turned it over to me, who sent it to the prime minister, who was in his office on Parliament Hill, and my memory is that it arrived in Ottawa weeks before the election. In Byzantium, this sort of thing was routine, but then, so is the Leader's version of it.

In the 1965 general election, things only went from bad to worse. Regrets multiply, along with recriminations. Actually, Byzantium's Leader should have won in 1965 — "I had done my best" — but treachery intervened: "Had the Honourable Duff Roblin been a candidate, I believe nothing could have stopped us."

On Saturday, 18 September, Diefenbaker met Roblin in Winnipeg, where Roblin "agreed to become a candidate." Roblin was promised a cabinet post and a leg up in the leadership race to run — "he was in his 40s while I was in my 70s" — but then, forty-eight hours later, Roblin refused.

What happened? Well, you would never guess. At least, I couldn't.

". . .I was not aware," the Leader now tells us, "of the messages and emissaries arriving in Winnipeg from Toronto with contrary advice. *I found out one year later* that Dalton Camp and George Hogan had arrived on the Sunday to argue Roblin out of running." Simply untrue.

In Byzantium, it is plain, people who were close to the Leader, and trusted by him, systematically, habitually and cheerfully lied to him. Part of the raging fever that was his constant temperature during those "tumultuous years" came from this daily injection of venomous falsehood administered by those he trusted.

It is, in the final analysis, sad.

Of Ontario's Premier John Robarts, in 1965: "Robarts did nothing to assist us. *I later discovered* he had been less than co-operative from the beginning."

Or this: "I do know that my instructions to our national campaign headquarters in Ottawa were not translated into effective action. The responsibility for this must rest with either Goodman, who was in charge, or Flora MacDonald, who was at headquarters and often in touch with Camp."

Or this: "McCutcheon, Goodman, Ernest Jackson, Harry Price could not have worked harder [against the Leader]. . .if they had been campaigning against an opposing party. John Bassett, however, was in a class by himself."

Or these:

"When I rose to speak [at the fateful party meeting in 1966], I discovered just how thorough Camp had been. For the regular podium, one had been substituted that would not hold my notes!"

"Premier [Robert L.] Stanfield appeared not to be displeased with the cold reception I was receiving. . ."

"G.W. Baldwin, MP. . . .was most annoyed that he had not been made a Minister."

"I had informed him [Roland Michener] many times that he was being undermined by the ideas of his Liberal 'Friends,' but he had never seen fit to agree. . ."

"Appointment to the Senate. . .seemed to lessen his [Grattan O'Leary's] sense of party responsibility. Indeed, in a speech to the Senate on the evening of December 1962, he devoted himself to building up the Opposition."

"About two or three the next morning, I received a telephone call from a distinguished former member of the press. . .[Defence Minister Douglas] Harkness was reported in a state of high exhilaration . . . After a few more rounds of refreshment he had agreed: 'I'll do it, I will resign tomorrow morning.' He did, but to his surprise it was no surprise to me. . ."

Paragraph upon paragraph, page after page, spilling over the covers — even into the *Toronto Sun*: "Nor can [Diefenbaker] forget the injuries inflicted on him by some members of his party," laments Joan Sutton, who quotes the Leader as saying: "I'm not even an honorary member of the Conservative Party because Mr. Camp wouldn't allow it. I've no position whatsoever. . ."

It is a pity he has not read his own party's constitution, which makes him a life member of the party's national executive (a body he has long despised), and which similarly recognized John Bracken and George Drew before him. More than a pity that he should suffer from so many self-inflicted wounds.

In Byzantium, there can be no figure more heroic than the man who goes into battle and falls upon his own sword.

The Globe & Mail, 11 February 1980

Clive Cocking, *Following the Leaders: A Media-Watcher's Diary of Campaign '79* (Doubleday).

"I have just spent two months with the national news media following the leaders on the campaign trail," Clive Cocking tells us, early on in his book. "My interest was not in the politicians. . .but in their devoted, ever-present retinue of reporters and columnists. I had gone out to observe the news media in their natural habitat. . . ."

But the "natural habitat" of the news media is not on the campaign trail, aboard the campaign jet, or in the campaign bus. Not any more than flying through Mach One upside down at thirty-thousand feet is the natural habitat of a fighter pilot. It's only that once in a while — and, please, not too often — that's where you might find yourself. If the campaign trail were the natural habitat of the news media, they'd all be dead.

Indeed, I suspect that, for most journalists, following the leaders on the campaign trail is an unnatural act. Not that they do it badly, but that it defies doing well, and everyone I have met along the way admits it.

This confusion of normal function and abnormal venue attends Cocking wherever he goes. For example, at a Joe Clark rally in Port Colborne: "Also I note one real concerned citizen (as opposed to party flunkies) in the crowd, an irate unemployed seaman who wants to know what Joe is going to do about the fact that half of Canada's 7,000 seamen are unemployed. . .A couple of reporters later ask the man some questions. How's he going to vote?

"But about the fact that we have such extreme unemployment among seamen in a country that lives by trade and that once had one of the largest merchant marine fleets in the world — no concern. It was news to me. In fact, my own latent journalistic interest was stimulated here, sensing a story that could be developed, one that intertwined politics and a real-life problem. Not so with the horde, impatient to get on with the next round of speechifying."

My own latent journalistic interest was stimulated here by the hunch (and we are only at page 93) that there is something wrong with this book — apart from the writing itself — and what's wrong with it is an overwhelming naïveté.

After following the media following the leaders for two months, Cocking sums up his experience:

"The campaign was one long media event. It has left this (drooping) media-watcher with some serious concerns about what is happening to our electoral process and the media's role in it. . . .Today the electoral process is no longer a dialogue, but a monologue — and the politicians are doing the talking through the media. What's worse. . . they're selling images, not policies."

Well, speaking of images, take a look at Cocking (page 78) on the occasion of his first day with the media accompanying Joe Clark:

"This is the first time I've seen Joe Clark up close in the (as it were) flesh. . . . Smaller, slighter than expected, and pudgier; he seems proud of his round little belly, constantly thrusting it forward. . . . Despite his conservative dark blue three-piece suit, he looks younger than thirty-nine. The way he speaks, drooping his chin, giving his voice deeper resonance and emphasizing his incipient jowls. . . ."

That's quite a first impression for a man anxious to intertwine politics with the problems of real life. There's more to come. Attending a rally at a Polish Community Cultural Centre, the media-watcher reports:

"The Tories are at least capable of getting out their supporters: that itself is a sign of good politics. Joe Baby (as I'm inclined to call him from time to time) lays on a little news tonight. . . .Otherwise the night's theme is much the same. The Poles are able to restrain themselves from exuberant dancing in the hall and the streets."

This book, you see, is about the news media and their passion for trivia, their shallowness, and their inability to sense a story, like the one about the unemployed seaman. Reading Cocking, I am reminded of the preacher who could deliver a good sermon on the evils of drink only when he was loaded.

The book is a treasury of trivia and a mine of deep-down shallowness — enough zingers, ribaldry, leering asides, vulgarisms, booze and dope to bring the mothers of Canada to their knees to pray their children be spared a career in journalism. If anything, Cocking's version of the news media on tour reminds me of a Press Gallery Annual Dinner, extended into infinity.

" 'I've never done anything low-key in my life,' he chuckles." That's Fred Ennis speaking — he's in radio — and fun-loving Fred goes on to say that he has "never done anything in this campaign or in 1974 he would be ashamed to have the whole world know — 'I get drunk, I shout at stewardesses.' " (Concluding a recent stewardess-shouting bout, good ole' boy Fred confides, "I tipped her a nickel and told her to vote Liberal.")

There is also a certain amount of Cocking-teasing going on here: the drinking is out in the open, and the media-watcher maintains a militant alert for pot, but then there's the question of — well — s-e-x. Do the news media do it?

"Arnie Patterson. . . spies a television reporter and his attractive lady seat companion, and quips: 'It's nice of you people to have your honeymoon on the bus.' Assistant press secretary Pat Gossage, a slight, wavy-haired youngish man in a rumpled hiking jacket, tugs at Arnie's sleeve, saying jokingly, 'Shhh. I told you about that — they're not the married couple.' Meaning?"

That's my question too — *meaning*?

Cocking suspected "media apprehensiveness" whenever he came near. One reporter asks him what he's going to report, or not report: "My answer: I'm covering this one big media event like a reporter and I'm going to report everything that seems significant and/or interesting."

" 'Even' — she asks — 'if you hear (and here names must be deleted) so-and-so is sleeping with so-and-so?' Picking myself carefully up off the floor, my complicated reply goes as follows: I hadn't heard; only use if it's relevant; *very* unlikely to use names; not really looking for this sort of thing."

The exchange plunges Cocking into rumination:

"Egad. Is sex, scandal and gossip all the news media have on their mind these days? Do they not know the difference between hearing

157

and *proving?*. . . An experience like this can throw a media-watcher into deep gloom."

Elsewhere, Cocking expands on the subject and, sort of, on his mission:

"Some clarification for the record. I had set out in the beginning as the quiet, unassuming observer whose concern was with campaign journalism; with the people, with the process and the result. What has happened shows how easy it is for reporters to become participants in the events they cover. As to matters sexual, my viewpoint (cleverly concealed so as not to spoil the fun) has always been very simple and straightforward. It is that the nation has no business in the bedrooms of the news media.

"However. If in the coming weeks I discover, say, Paul Whitelaw locked in a compromising position with some well-connected lady. . .

"Enough. What are the papers saying?"

Putting pillow-talk aside, and it ain't easy, Cocking is a quick observer of the passing scene, media-wise:

"Not all of these reporters resemble insurance agents. The archetypal reporter still exists: I glimpsed one of these near-extinct creatures awhile ago. . . He was a rumpled, baggy-eyed veteran wire service man with a lined, hang-dog face — and with a bottle wrapped in a newspaper tucked under his arm."

On page 64, we meet "the silver-haired *Toronto Star* writer, Val Sears," who reappears, on page 88, as "the *Toronto Star*'s veteran campaigner, Val Sears. . . Fiftyish, with silvery hair and smooth pink features, he has the droll manner of a man. . . about to burst forth with his latest witticism."

You can tell Cocking admires Sears; you can also tell he does not admire Allan Fotheringham, who "must accept the blame for thrusting me, stammering and blushing, into the limelight." Fotheringham, you see, poked fun at Cocking's assignment even before the media-watcher mounted his first bus. For that, he'll be sorry:

"Allan Fotheringham. . .stomps in out of the snow, his short round body wrapped in a corduroy trenchcoat, accompanied by an attractive lady in a fur hat. . . ."

You get the picture? Now for the details:

"As to Fotheringham, the man, what is known? He is well-fed. . . He is a natty, if inconsistent, dresser. On some occasions he's inclined to wear a velvet suit, on others a seersucker suit: showing contradictory tendencies of trendy foppishness and American tourist informality.

"But what of Fotheringham the writer? He is, first, a stylist fascinated by the sight of public figures. There is, in fact, evidence of an obsession with fashion and grooming."

I could go on. So could you. Cocking does!

"There's some action at the bar too. En route there, a brief chat with George Oake, who tells me, 'I find you don't have time to get into trouble. By the end of the day you're so tired, you just flake out.'

"Did I ask him about his nocturnal habits? No. Why are they saying these things to me?"

Because, Clive, a lot of them were putting you on. As one of them since wrote me:

"What Cocking missed was quite basic — 'Being spoofed.' One would think, in an age of simple understanding, that Cocking would understand. But that's life."

This book is one long leg-pull, frequently interrupted by bad writing ("This building is itself a tacky structure with a most nervous-making hesitant elevator") and by woolly assertion ("I know now why Toronto drama and variety people fly out to Vancouver so often to use the sumptuous new studios there: it's easier on the nerves"). What it will tell you about the media, media politics and political campaigns will not get you far in journalism school.

Still, you can't say Cocking wasn't warned. At the start of his argosy, one reporter told him: "I just don't think you're going to see much. Everybody is too busy. You're just not going to see anyone screwing a stewardess in the back of the plane."

"There are times," Cocking concludes, "when being a media-watcher is depressing."

How about how I feel, a media-reader reading what a media-watcher wrote about what he watched? Egad.

The news media follow the leaders in campaigns because, like it or not, "speechifying" is at the heart of the democratic process. Policy proclaimed, or explained, is the prerogative of the leaders; what they say, or don't say, is basic to the campaign, as it has been, and ever shall be.

That the assignment is also boring much of the time is not the fault of the media, nor even of the politicians, but because the practical options and choices in our politics are so few. Although following the leaders is essential to the coverage, no one promised it would be either exciting or profound. That the coverage is often "shallow," as Cocking claims, is true only if one admits to the fundamental shallowness of the exercise, which is only to say that, if our politics were somehow different, so would be the coverage.

Finally, what of the bizarre conduct of the media "horde," as so relentlessly revealed by the author? The tensions aboard the campaign jet are considerable: one lives in constant proximity not only to one's adversaries, the politicians, but to one's competitors. Those who drink are inclined to drink more — there being more occasion for it and, as well, the rounds are free. Those who do dope, do. Those who swear find they have more to curse. And, of course, boors will always be boors, especially when they have a captive audience. What Cocking fails to see is that life on the campaign trail makes for parody, which is a far cry from reality.

Saturday Night, March 1980

Barbara Amiel, *Confessions* (Macmillan)

In 1955, her family moved from Hamilton to St. Catharines.

"I did not go with them," writes Barbara Amiel. "I had no choice but to try living on my own — after all, I was already a grown woman of fourteen."

So she rented a room "occupied by a garage mechanic and his family," later moved into a basement "apartment" in a house owned by a Pole, went to high school, took jobs after school, made friends, and began writing, as the school correspondent for the St. Catharines *Standard* and as editor of the school yearbook. She made out, although "Trading a knack for writing sentences to get by in life doesn't reveal an especially admirable character."

Perhaps not. Still, the force and facility of Barbara Amiel's prose does reveal a *strong* character — resilient, self-reliant, uncompromising, fiercely independent. Indeed, halfway through her book, I gave up marking the pages with queries, notes and underlinings, and loped to the end simply admiring the view. To give you an idea, it reads something like William F. Buckley out of Ayn Rand by Harold Laski.

It was Laski, who was so often outrageous, who described the role of the social critic: "to prick people into the insurgency of thought." If *Confessions* doesn't do this to you, then you are not paying attention.

Barbara Amiel, somewhat a libertarian, briefly an Anglican, a lapsed socialist, an elitist, a skilled polemicist, the most compleat liberal since the closing of the Manchester school, is a competent journalist. And she can write. Which reminds me of the comment by an American liberal on the late Westbrook Pegler, whose newspaper columns regularly savaged trade union leaders, New Dealers, Eleanor Roosevelt, and other liberal sacred cows: "I just wish," he said wistfully, "the son of a bitch was on our side."

Amiel's targets are the "left-libbers," feminists, multiculturalists, the legions of do-gooders who proliferate and populate "the nanny state." Her book is, in part, a recounting of the author's encounters with her prey — anyone or anything seeming to threaten her personal liberty. And in spite of the caveat — "I am not a philosopher, only a journalist" — *Confessions* is both autobiography and, for want of a better word, auto-philosophy. With the latter, I had some difficulty, not to say occasional, and profound, disagreement.

But when Amiel engages the Human Rights Commissions of both Manitoba and Ontario (each had objected to her use of the word "Hun" in an article about postwar Britain), she is not only right, and convincingly so, but downright appealing. I will not spoil it for you, other than to report a clean kill by Amiel of a lot of bull, for which, from me, she earns the ears, the tail and a standing ovation. *Olé!*

There are other delights: a CBC poll of delegate voting intentions aired before the Liberal leadership convention which ultimately elected Pierre Trudeau, and which was dutifully and desperately rigged by Amiel to please her superiors (the poll "predicted" Trudeau); a harrowing overseas junket as a representative of international Communist youth; the advice of a Liberal MP who, when asked by Amiel how she could find out if the RCMP had a file on her, suggested she become an informer; a story on women "ripping off" the Unemployment Insurance Commission, which *Chatelaine* commissioned her to write, but which was never published. And more, including cameo impressions of Hollywood, Ann Margret, and Jane Fonda.

But sometimes the flow of logic rising from the rush of "confession" seems to be as lunatic as it is inexorable: "At the time I had my own abortion, I believed it to be morally wrong. . . I was in too much of a hurry with life. I couldn't wait the extra four months and then, if a child was 'inconvenient' for me, put it up for adoption. I chose murder instead."

Then: "I have no sentimental feelings about the child I killed. But I find my reasons morally reprehensible."

And finally: "But as I would not shrink from murder to protect my vital interests, I would not shrink from abortion — except I prefer to face what I am doing."

Now, all this is unequivocally tough, perhaps defiant, but still confusing — the confusion, in this instance, being the difference between an abortion for the sake of convenience, and one to protect a vital interest. As to an abortion of convenience: "If a man does not wish his wife or girlfriend to have a child because the financial burden will inconvenience him — for considerably longer than nine months — the mother should either be required to have an abortion or, if this is not acceptable to her, then the man should be released from financial responsibility for the child. Convenience is not a one-way street."

I confess here that I am entirely lost. Still, to be fair, we are dealing with an hypothesis. *If* there were abortion on demand; *if* the father would be inconvenienced by the birth of a child; *if* the mother refused an abortion; *then*. . . .

But the argument loses me because, I thought, Amiel was *against* coercion and *for* personal responsibility, such as the acute responsibility of a girlfriend's boyfriend. Or is that a one-way street?

Sometimes, too, the auto-philosophy seems cavalier, even silly: "Most people do not become drunk when they drink — and if they do, they throw up nicely and go to bed. Since it would never occur to me to prevent all those people who enjoy their two gins-and-tonic a day from indulging in their little vice in order to protect the minority who can't stop at that, it would seem similarly improper to prevent anyone who wishes to use drugs from doing so in order to save the drug-abuser himself. This seems an inappropriate principle on which to make social policy in a free country. All one can do is legalize everything, then hold everyone responsible for their behaviour while under the influence of an intoxicant."

Thus — sure enough — the drunken driver who killed a pedestrian could not plead manslaughter but would be charged with murder. The difficulty I have with all this tidy libertarian permissiveness, in a society set upon by everyone charged with their own responsibility while loaded up on booze and mescalin, is — dare I mention it? — that the victims have been omitted from the equation. I do not mean only the employers, families, neighbours, and the agencies of the law, all overtaxed already, but those who would soon be dead, maimed, mugged, or otherwise maltreated by these fresh hordes of liberated trippers.

"I am a wandering Jew," writes Barbara Amiel. "My allegiance is not to any piece of earth. . . My allegiance is to ideas, and most especially the extraordinary idea of individual liberty. The idea is still there in the North American landscape, a landscape I have come to love. I do not wish to leave. But my suitcase is packed."

Okay. But should this "extraordinary idea of individual liberty" become so indivisible as to exclude social conscience, a concern for life, and a sense of responsibility for others, then I'm packing a suitcase and *I'm* leaving.

The Globe & Mail, 20 September 1980

Jeffrey Simpson, *Discipline of Power* (Personal Library)

I used to say about Canadian politics that the subject was never so dull as were so many who wrote about it. That politics seems much more interesting to more Canadians these days is a debt owed to people like Peter Newman, George Bain, Dick Beddoes, Geoffrey Stevens, Allan Fotheringham, Marjorie Nichols and the editorial board of the *Globe and Mail*, among others. Of them all, I would think Bain's contribution has been the greatest. His Ottawa columns made page 6 of the *Globe and Mail* an institution in Canadian journalism, one which Stevens has duly maintained.

Writing effectively about Canadian politics, to a readership with at least an approximate idea of the subject's true relevance and importance, is often the sheer triumph of style over substance. In this multi-media age, those obliged to write about our politics are addressing readers who have been sated with information from an invisible universe of satellites and who already know more than they really care to know. If writers are to stuff them with still more information — about, let us say, constitutional renewal or the law of the seas — they had better have some wit and style at their command.

The failure of *Discipline of Power* lies in its flawed style, which leads a reader to the conclusion that it was too hurriedly written or that the author had considerable difficulty in his first attempt to break out of journalism into literature. Perhaps it was something of both. But he appears not to have heard of Charles Lamb's advice to aspiring writers: "Kill your darlings!" Trying, for instance, to grasp the meaning of a Simpson simile is like trying to carry water in a sieve: "Entering federal-provincial relations without experience is like being lost in Harlem with pocketfuls of cash." "If there was to be a 'fresh face on federalism,' Gordon Robertson was not the man to apply the make-up." "Telling Crosbie. . . to absorb Petro Canada's debt was like asking Hannibal to call off his march on Rome." "Now, that might have been a sharp point on which to hang the Liberal Party's credibility in power, but Trudeau immediately varnished the point with qualifications." "Clark has everywhere battled his own image reflected in the cracked mirror of television." "The Liberal candidates appearing with Trudeau in the commercials were there to scatter the limelight from Trudeau." "Clark struggled against Trudeau in Quebec like a heretic denouncing the Pope." "As festering national problems threatened to become open sores, politicians protected their own skins without worrying much about the health of the nation." Or, a personal favourite: "They [the Conservatives] were like marathon swimmers who, having finally reached the other side of the lake, collapsed in sweet ecstasy, forgetting the chill of the air until just before they were frozen stiff."

I suppose there is really nothing terribly wrong about any of this, but there is nothing quite right about any of it either. The image of Peter Lougheed "pulling together the wagons for a fight with the federal Government" hovers between a cliché and a malapropism. To write "There was nothing sinister nor partisan" is merely bad grammar, but also a pity, because the author was on his way to a thoughtful conclusion.

Nor are the aphorisms especially apt: "Illusions are the perverted dreams of politics," he writes, "but they are essential to any leader trying to create the impression of momentum." It is one of those sentences in which the subject and predicate are interchangeable and will still mean as much.

Or: "Reputations are quick to harden and slow to melt."

It may be that the NDP's youthful organizer, Robin Sears, was resented by the older hands of the party. But a "snotty upstart"? And was Trudeau's appointment of Marc Lalonde to the energy portfolio "a gauntlet thrown at Alberta"? *At?*

Another of the author's short suits is dialogue, evidenced by this reported conversation between Eugene Whelan, Herb Gray and friends:

> "We can't vote for that budget. It's too hard on low-and-middle-class Canadians," said Gray with customary seriousness.
>
> "Wait until the farmers hear about that excise tax," Whelan chimed in, his double chin quivering as he chuckled at the thought.
>
> Similar talk was everywhere, and Steven Gouge could not believe what he was hearing.
>
> "They've gone crazy. I can't believe it. Why are they doing this?" he asked his dinner companions. None of them had attended the Wednesday morning meeting of the Liberal caucus and so groped for a reply.

And I am groping for a way of expressing my approval of Simpson, the diligent journalist and thoughtful observer of our political processes, while upholding the right of every reader to be given something other than semolina as food for thought. I agree with much of what Simpson has written and am grateful to him for stimulating further notions in my mind as to what — apart from everything — went wrong with the government of Joe Clark. I just hope he will, next time, put things better.

I need no more tell you what *Discipline Of Power* is about than I need explain the story-line of the Book of Genesis. The author and I share the same curiosity about the 257 days of the recent Tory interregnum, not only as to *what* happened, but why. Even so, I have the uneasy feeling that Simpson has written about a subject most Canadians least want to read.

Loyal Tories who read this book may find it induces apoplexy: others, more objective — Liberals, for example — may find it amusing, although the author plainly does not. For students of politics, however, there is much here to think about, including Simpson's principal thesis which, baldly stated, is that the Conservative Party, having been too long in opposition, came to office lacking the discipline required to wield power. There is, then, a fateful inevitability, a self-destruct mechanism of the party's own creation in the works, which makes for a short, unhappy tenure.

Certainly, the mechanism was in place from the outset of Clark's brief tenure as prime minister. Opposition parties, Simpson argues, come to believe their own rhetoric, which is bad enough, and also to believe in their own expedient politics, which is worse. When they arrive in office and are then confronted by what might be called the facts of life, there is an immediate collision between the partisan world of their own making and the real world of power and responsibility. For Clark and his colleagues, the collision was obviously traumatic.

As to that, there is a wealth of documentation provided out of Simpson's research. He is likely the leading authority on this curious footnote to our political history. Anyway, the story of the Clark administration is, by definition, neither a lengthy one nor, Simpson maintains, a happy one in its implications for political institutions.

I do have certain reservations, or arguments, about some of his conclusions. I have been told, for example, that Lougheed cautioned Clark — Tory to Tory — that he should proceed more slowly with his Draconian national energy policy, indeed, to proceed one year at a time. As well, that when Lougheed learned of the eighteen-cent increase in the excise tax, he remarked to himself, "I hope these fellows know what they're doing." I only know that because I heard it from Lougheed.

Simpson has it that Alberta's premier put the screws on Clark and turned them each time they met in negotiations. Meanwhile, Ontario's Bill Davis had gone public with his case against the proposed federal energy package which — if you can follow this — had been put forward by Clark's energy minister, who did not have the prime minister's complete confidence, as proposed by that minister's deputy, whom Clark's policy advisor wanted fired. Shades of Diefenbaker!

And when it was all over, Simpson informs us, the defeated prime minister summoned the senior members of the bureaucracy and tendered them his grateful thanks for their services, whereupon they gave him a standing ovation.

If Simpson's prose had been equal to his research, this would have been a marvellous book. Even so, the subject-matter is so painful that it might still not have been much easier to read.*

*Notwithstanding, Mr. Simpson's book won the Governor General's award for Non-Fiction.